New British Wine

New Makers
New Flavours
New Ethos

Written and compiled by Abbie Moulton
Photographed by Maria Bell

Hoxton Mini Press

New British Wine
First edition

Published in 2023 by Hoxton Mini Press, London.

The cover is printed on Favini Crush, an eco-friendly paper
made with 15 percent grape waste.

*Except photography: p.10, p.25, p.35, p.44, p.46 (image on left), pp. 50–51,
p.111, p.113, pp.120-123, pp.159-160, p.163 (top and left image) © Lesley Lau;
Westwell's vineyard on pp.16–17 © Sam Scales; Grape picking at Forty Hall on
p.109 © Pablo Antoli; Westwell Ortega Skin-Contact on p.119 © Galia Pike /
Westwell Wines; The Ethicurean garden on pp.214-215 © Iain Pennington.

Design by Alex Hunting, additional design and illustrations by Richard Mason,
project-editing and copy-editing by Octavia Stocker, proofreading by Gaynor
Sermon, production by Sarah-Louise Deazley, production and research support
by Alison Evans. A special thanks to Beca Jones for coming up with the idea for
this book.

A CIP catalogue record for this book is available from the British Library.

ISBN: 978-1-914314-23-0

Printed and bound by OZGraf, Poland

Hoxton Mini Press is an environmentally conscious publisher, committed
to offsetting our carbon footprint. This book is 100% carbon compensated,
with offset purchased from Stand For Trees.

For every book you buy from our website, we plant a tree:
www.hoxtonminipress.com

Contributors

WRITTEN BY
ABBIE MOULTON

Abbie Moulton is a drinks writer, broadcaster and presenter, specialising in wine and whisky – the people who make them and the places that pour them. Her work has been featured in the *Evening Standard, The Times* and *Suitcase* magazine, among other publications, and she regularly chats on the radio and on podcasts.

While a dedicated researcher of London's many bars and restaurants, she's happiest in wellies, whether on vineyards or farmyards. She'll never say no to a glass of chilled red.

PHOTOGRAPHED BY
MARIA BELL

Maria Bell is a freelance photographer based between the Isle of Wight and London. Her career documenting food and farming has seen her work alongside the industry's top chefs and restaurants and featured in national newspapers and books. In 2021, she was shortlisted for the Food Photographer of the Year award.

Photographing this book has been the perfect chance to visualise the produce-led, nature-friendly wine industry that sees her hopeful for the future.

Locations

Tillingham (p.42)

Lola Provisions (p.62)

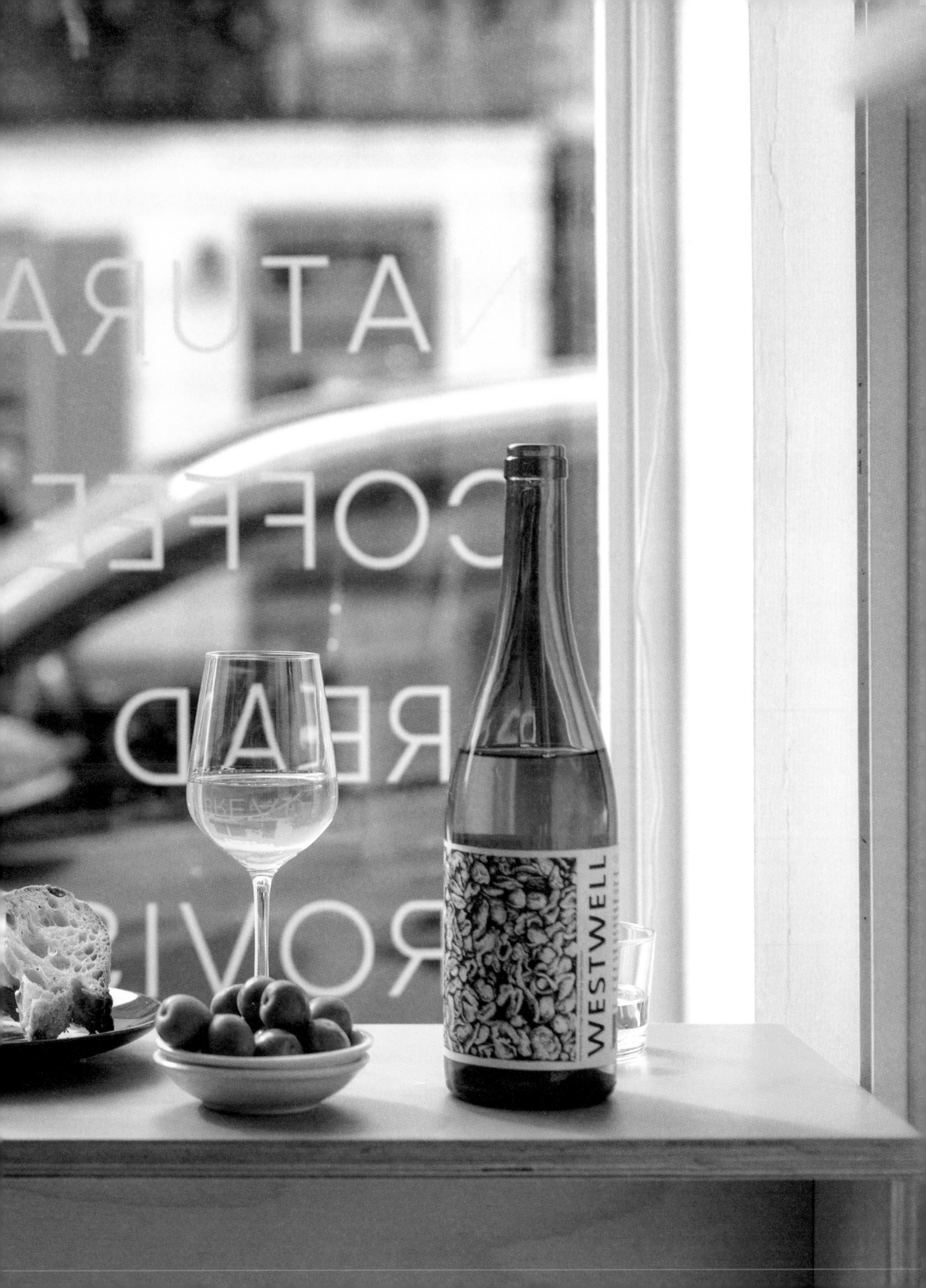
WESTWELL

Dominic Smith (p.38)

OPPOSITE
Bench (p.146)

Westwell (p.118)

Introduction

New British Wine: beyond old pulp

If you've heard the term 'British wine' then you might already be wincing. It has a dubious reputation, and specifically describes a rather crude and rudimentary drink (barely) popularised in the 20th century, made from imported grape concentrate – rehydrated, fermented and then bottled in the UK – that tends to be low in quality, low in price and usually found on the lowest shelf of the supermarket. The new kind of British wine that this book celebrates, one that's grown and produced in Britain, could not be more different.

British wine has come a long way in recent decades – and it's time we reclaim the term. You might already know that bright and elegant sparkling wines made in the south-east of England have begun to scoop up awards that once belonged to Champagne. What you might not know is that there is a burgeoning scene of winemakers, growers and sommeliers who are breaking away from familiar styles, making the most of being part of a region as yet unbound by bureaucracy or tradition. British wine is on the cusp of a new wave as new makers, new methods, new cultures, and yes, dare we say it, a new climate, have kickstarted a radical shift in how we produce, drink and think about wine. British food has already had its revolution, now it's time for British wine.

The long and varied history of winemaking on these islands dates back to the Roman times, when occupying soldiers planted vines and made a sweet honey-wine to remind them of home, but for the purposes of this book our story begins in the 1960s and 1970s, which are recognised by many as being the 'first wave' of British wine. The beginnings of the scene thriving today can be traced back to those post-war years when hobbyists and smallholders began planting plots of modern German varieties. The wines could often be unforgivingly thin and astringent; the vines, hardy hybrids bred by crossing European and North American grapevines were valued for their ability to ripen in Blighty's chilly climate and not, perhaps, for their flavour (although there were early flashes of brilliance and, in the right hands, many hybrid varieties can produce moreish results). This first wave wasn't making award-winning wine, but it was inventive and gutsy, and if the wines weren't always that tasty, well, at least we were having a go.

It wasn't until the late 1980s that things really began to look up. The second wave of British winemaking came into view when a couple of forward-thinking American winemakers, realised that southern England had the perfect conditions, from climate to soil (in fact, the very same chalk that lies beneath Champagne also forms the bedrock of Kent, Hampshire and Sussex), for making sparkling wine. Those winemakers founded Nyetimber in Sussex and, in 1998, their sparkling wine was crowned the Best Sparkling Wine in the World at the prestigious International Wine and Spirits Competition. Suddenly, high-quality, complex and mineral-rich sparkling from Britain was being celebrated on the world stage. Several other vineyards – Ridgeview, Chapel Down, Gusbourne

> '**People are pushing boundaries,
> doing things differently and exploring...
> in a few years the UK will be making the most
> innovative and interesting wine in the world.**'

ALEX HURLEY, WINEMAKER AT LONDON CRU

and Hattingley Valley, to name a few – joined the trail that Nyetimber blazed with equally jaw-dropping results.

The corks of British sparkling wine are still popping today. Sales are soaring, exports are up, vineyard plantings have tripled and even the Champagne houses are getting in on the action, buying up land and putting down roots on this side of the Channel. Today, about 70 percent of all wine produced in Britain is sparkling.

While Champagne-rivalling sparklings continue to dazzle, an emerging wave of winemakers are doing things differently: reviving those forgotten grape varieties and looking to ancient winemaking techniques. This book is about a new wave of British wine and the new generation taking the expert techniques and new-found knowledge of the second wave and combining it with the experimental attitude and hybrid grapes of the first. There's so much more to British wine than you might expect, and this book will take you on a tour of the best vineyards, producers, bars and bottle shops leading the way.

LEFT:
P. Franco (p.104) is an all-in-one bottle shop, bar and restaurant on east London's Lower Clapton Road. Founded in 2014 by Liam Kelleher and James Noble, the men behind the Noble Fine Liquor bottle shops (see Stockists). Will Gee, Paris Barghchi and Fred Clelland enjoy a glass of Field Notes from Offbeat (p.196).

NEW MAKERS

We might not have the history and heritage of traditional regions, where generations of farmers have handed down the secrets of viticultural knowledge to their children and grandchildren, but experience can be earned. Many of the winemakers in these pages have returned to Britain after working abroad for many years, or travelled here to pastures new, like Blackbook's Californian founder Sergio Verrillo (p.54) who makes extraordinary-quality still wines from Essex-grown Chardonnay and Pinot Noir in a winery (which means a place where wine is made) on an industrial estate in Battersea. Some, like Alex Hurley, the winemaker at another brilliant urban winery London Cru (p.152), were first drawn to the UK after discovering Champagne-style English sparkling, but have now found themselves part of a community of makers and growers who are pushing boundaries and developing unique styles.

Unbound by the shackles of the rules and regulations that exist in older regions, producers in Britain are free to experiment, and many are grabbing that freedom by the barrel. Winemakers like Ben Walgate at Tillingham (p.42) or Daniel Ham at Offbeat (p.196) left careers at larger commercial producers to launch their own independent wineries where they could apply their technical know-how to more playful, far less prescriptive styles of their own. It is this range and potential of British wine that is fast attracting eminent winemakers from all over the world.

NEW METHODS

The last decade has seen a rise in the popularity of low-intervention winemaking. Contemporary, conventional winemaking can often rely on heavy-handed interventions to steer the wine towards a desired outcome, or correct any faults that might develop, whether it's by adding sugar to increase the alcohol content or using lab-grown yeasts to guide a wine into a particular flavour profile. Many of the new wave of British winemakers prefer to take a step back and wait to see how the grapes or juice develop before deciding whether they'll make a clear sparkling rosé or a cloudy pét-nat (an affably frothy variant of sparkling wine that's become cultishly popular thanks to its easy-drinking nature and spectrum of styles – it's short for *pétillant naturel,* which translates to 'natural sparkling' in French. For more information see the Glossary), rather than forcing it into a style that it might not suit. Several of the winemakers and sommeliers I spoke to referred to this as 'following the wine'.

This style of low-intervention winemaking is also known as 'natural wine'. Natural wine is a complex and divisive topic that I will brutally simplify as 'grapes grown and wines made with little to no chemical or technological intervention'. It's controversial partly because it's an unregulated term, so it is possible for commercially produced bottles to masquerade as 'natural wine'. But its critics also argue that natural wines can sometimes contain the kind of undesirable, sour or musty flavours that traditional winemakers have spent decades learning how to avoid.

Others, however, would say that wine *should* be more varied and less processed. Heavy-handed, industrial winemaking is not only unsustainable, it's just not as exciting or surprising and, to many, not nearly as delicious. While I didn't set out to write about natural wines, many of the winemakers and restaurateurs spoke of their respect for the land and love for locally sourced ingredients, and

so it follows that the wines in this book tend to lean towards this style. As Caroline Dubois at Isca Wines (p.74) says, 'For me, wine is like food. It's fermented grape juice. People are more aware of organic fruit and vegetables, but not so much about what they drink. That is changing.'

NEW CLIMATE

We can't talk about British wine without acknowledging the climate crisis because, without the climate crisis, there might not be any British wine at all; agriculture, and therefore viticulture, in Europe is shifting north as temperatures rise. In 2021 Bordeaux, a winemaking region famously rigid in its rules and restrictions, approved six new varieties more able to stand the heat due to fears that, one day, the classic varieties they're known for will no longer be able to thrive there. And Champagne houses are purchasing land in southern England, not just because it's perfect for vines but also, perhaps, because they fear that one day Champagne as a region might not be.

For the moment, however, the islands that make up Britain are still on the outer limits, the furthest latitude north, where grape growing is possible. Any further, and it's just too cold for vines to put out good fruit. But Britain is in a sweet spot, where the grapes ripen, but not too much, retaining a freshness and enlivening acidity in the glass that warmer regions covet. Our drizzly summers do pose a challenge, creating the perfect conditions for vine-suffocating mildews and moulds to flourish, while the threat of late spring frost doesn't help either. It's not easy, but for those growers and winemakers brave and bold enough to try, the rewards when they succeed far outweigh the risk.

The real issue that vineyards face in terms of our climate, however, isn't wet or cold weather – it's the unpredictability. Each annual crop of grapes harvested is called, in wine terms, a vintage. In Britain, vintage variation is extreme. In the last few years alone, we've seen record highs and plummeting lows. 2018 was a bumper crop across the UK, a rare 'wonder vintage', but then, in 2021, a cool summer and endless rain resulted in a 'lost vintage' in which some were unable to make any wines at all. While most vineyards are in some way protected from this variation, those that are farmed sustainably and organically are more exposed to the elements.

RIGHT:
Grapes are harvested at Westwell (p.118), a vineyard on the chalk slopes of the Pilgrims' Way in Kent where they grow Chardonnay, Pinot Noir, Pinot Meunier, Ortega and a little sprinkling of Rondo. Westwell now has 34 acres under vine and over 50,000 vines.

NEW ETHOS

Even though it makes running a vineyard riskier, sustainability is crucial to the story of new British wine. There is a resounding dedication among the vignerons in this book to future-focused responsible farming. Change is happening, and it starts from the ground up. Consumers and producers are waking up to the damage industrial practices have caused, from monocultures creating a lack of biodiversity to pesticides and chemicals depleting the soil of nutrients.

In the British wine industry, organic and regenerative farming was pioneered by winemakers and vineyards like Will Davenport (p.68) in the 1990s, then carried on by Forty Hall (p.108), and Oxney (p.98) in more recent years. There are even biodynamic vineyards in Britain, like Ancre Hill (p.78) and Domaine Hugo (p.196), which put into practice quasi-mystical, lunar calendar-led methods developed in the 1920s. One of the earliest organic agricultural movements, biodynamic methods aim to regenerate the land and bolster diversity by eschewing all man-made chemicals and doing as much by hand as possible. The grapes that vineyards working organically or biodynamically produce can be purer and more flavourful than anything grown with conventional methods. It takes guts to run a vineyard in the UK – and even more so to do it organically. But we're a plucky bunch, and that is worth raising a glass to.

TOP:
Young vines at Botley Farm, a biodynamic vineyard where Hugo Williams cultivates Chardonnay, Pinot Meunier, Pinot Noir, Pinot Gris and Pinot Blanc for Domaine Hugo and Offbeat (p.196).

MIDDLE:
Winemaker Daniel Ham at Offbeat (p.196) tends to his vines, his background in marine biology gives him a scientific approach to low-intervention winemaking.

BOTTOM:
A bottle of Ancestral Red, a fizzy red wine made by Matt Gregory, aka The English Winemaker, (p.202) from vines grown in the Leicestershire Wolds.

NEW FLAVOURS

New British wine is about embracing and celebrating its unique terroir. And what British wine is most known for is its lively, bracing acidity that lends an impressive zippiness to our sparkling and still wines. This high level of acidity is something that producers aiming to make more recognisable French-style wines might want to wrestle with, although some winemakers, like Blackbook (p.54) and Trevibban Mill (p.184), are already showing that classic still wines with a real softness and depth can absolutely be made here. Other winemakers are doing wonderful things with Bacchus, a modern vine that's earning a reputation as Britain's signature grape because of its popularity with growers and wine judges; its notes of elderflower, ripe apple and hedgerow are happily reminiscent of an overgrown English orchard.

Another grape that has done well in Britain is Seyval Blanc, a modern variety that is banned in France because it's not a pure *vitis vinifera* (European grapevine) but instead a cross between European and North American vines. Here, it seems to thrive and can make vivid, spicy wines that are a little more punchy and a little less poised than a Bacchus or Chardonnay, but perhaps all the more interesting for it. Ortega, a German grape variety, is also being used to make distinctly British wines, like Tillingham's Endgrain (p.49), a bright, green-gold wine with notes of stone fruits, and at Westwell (p.118) it is fermented at a low temperature in stainless steel to draw out precise, floral notes as well as its distinctive peachiness. But none of these new, uniquely British flavours would be possible if there wasn't an audience out there willing to try wines coming from smaller producers using lesser-known grapes.

NEW CULTURE

It's not just the wine – it's also the wine *culture* that has undergone a massive revolution in the last decade. No longer stuffy, starched and formal with intimidating wine lists, there's a growing movement of bars and bottle shops that are relaxed and light-filled with friendly service, great soundtracks and short, dynamic wine lists that change depending on season and availability.

These places are owned and run by people who want to support local, homegrown producers. Lee Coad, one of the co-founders of the seafood restaurant Angela's (p.132) in Margate, lists British wine because, as he says, 'it feeds into our ethos of keeping it local and reducing waste... It gives our restaurants a context, a sense of place.' Many of the bar owners, sommeliers and chefs I spoke to have close relationships with nearby vineyards, often visiting the growers and getting to know their wines before bringing them back to share with their customers. Paris Barghchi at P. Franco (p.104) has toiled through harvest with Offbeat (p.196), and Sven-Hanson Britt, the chef and owner of Oxeye (p.190), spent weeks driving up and down the whole country, visiting vineyards with his sommelier Ben, to create a wine list that features hundreds of bottles of British wine.

Fresh approaches have flung open the doors to a new generation who are passionate about provenance and sustainability, and also have a taste for the lower alcohol levels often found with cool-climate wines (as the grapes contain less sugar for the yeasts to convert into alcohol). At Lola Provisions (p.62), owner Katie has found that most people 'get excited by these wines... they appreciate the work that goes into the bottle, and accept that the price can be higher. Some can take a bit more convincing, but once they've tasted a glass or two, in all honesty there's no going back.' With a widening demographic comes a whole new lexicon – ditching old lingo for more playful terms, where easy-drinking wine becomes 'smashable juice' – a far cry from the esoteric language used by old-school sommeliers. You can love it or hate it but, as Brodie Meah from London-based wine bar Top Cuvée (p.114) puts it, 'Anything we can do to make the wine scene more approachable? We want to do that.'

WHAT'S NEXT?

British vineyards have found their groove with traditional-method sparkling wine and that's not going anywhere any time soon. Now a new wave of still wine and experimental sparkling styles are bringing in fresh flavours to explore. Will bottles from the UK one day be as ubiquitous on lists around the world as those of other, newer regions like South Africa, Chile or New Zealand? In time, it's possible, although as a small island our production will never match that of larger New World regions. But perhaps that's not a bad thing – it's always good to be in demand.

As the reputation of British wine grows, it is inevitable that rules and regulations will begin to follow. We are at a unique moment in time. Winemakers can still experiment with whatever grape variety or method they want, while a tug-of-war between freedom and discipline goes on behind the scenes. But more influential than any regulation is the future of the British climate. We have seen some truly spectacular vintages in the last few years. If Britain continues to warm, the styles of wine we'll be able to produce will continue to grow richer, fuller-bodied and more age-worthy. Will there be Champagne-style wine being made in Scotland one day? Maybe, but that implies a rather scary future. As temperatures rise, the weather will become more erratic and so, yes, grapes will bask in the sun, but they might also suffer from severe spring frosts and flash floods.

Today, British wine is radical, curious, creative and supremely delicious. The new wave is a movement being led by modern-day farmers determined to make wine in a way that won't destroy our planet, as well as visionaries developing styles that are uniquely British. It's defiant and boundary-pushing, full of grit, charm and soul. And it's only just getting started.

RIGHT:
Pressed grapes ferment at Renegade (p.140), an urban winery in east London. Fermentation is often done in open vessels, as oxygen helps the yeasts to multiply and convert the sugars to alcohol.

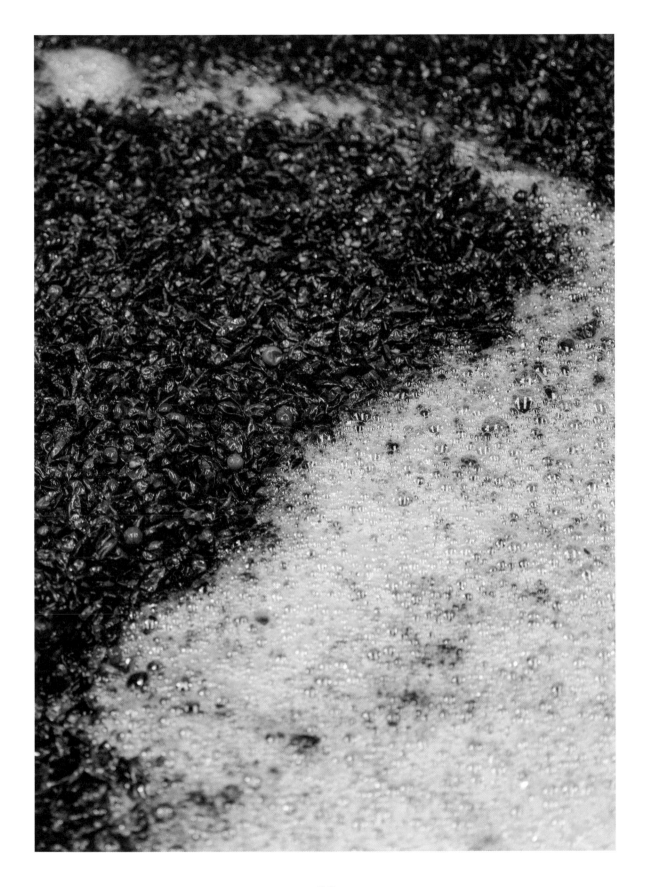

29

Industry

Voices

The vigneron using old vines to make new wine

The Grower: Tim Wildman

Tim Wildman's Lost Vineyard Preservation Society is working to revive Britain's abandoned vineyards. The winemaker and Master of Wine (a highly-respected qualification only awarded to the most knowledgeable vinologists) has spent years driving around the countryside, scouring fields and peering over hedges to find overgrown and forgotten vineyards, and in doing so, reveal clues about the UK's past.

Tim wanted to make wine in Britain, but he was also keen to break free from what he calls 'carbon copy Champagne' that's so popular today. 'Before the 1990s, it was mostly white table wine made from German varieties by hobbyists on really small-scale, tiny plots. We were starting to see some commercial vineyards by then, but in the 1970s and 1980s it was mostly people planting in their gardens and making wine in their sheds. The quality... let's say it was "variable"', he says with a grin. 'They tended to be early ripening varieties, planted specifically for the cooler climate – all the Schönburger, Madeleine Angevine, and so on.' It's these forgotten vineyards that Tim's reviving – preserving their status and resurrecting the Germanic grapes planted decades ago, now coined by Tim as 'heritage varieties'.

One of Tim's discoveries is a two-acre terraced vineyard, cut into the side of a slate valley in North Wales. Its steep terraces are reminiscent of those found in the Mosel or the Douro, and unseen (or as yet undiscovered) anywhere else in the UK. It was also planted with a medley of aromatic 'heritage' varieties that Tim was eager to work with: Rondo, Ortega, Solaris, Regent, Frühburgunder, Madeleine Angevine, Seyval Blanc and Dornfelder.

With these grapes, Tim has bottled his Lost in a Field Frolic pét-nat, made by Daniel Ham from Offbeat (p.196), blending rediscovered grapes from vineyards across England and Wales. The 2021 vintage is an exuberant foam party of Fruit Salad chews and sherbet. It is an alchemic blend of old varieties and new styles, one which encourages winemakers to embrace the vines that thrive so well here. Fun, inventive and heavenly to drink, it's a great example of what might be next for new British wine.

The winemaker breaking free from tradition

The Winemaker: Maheshika Bertin

It was perhaps inevitable that Maheshika Bertin would become a winemaker. Although born in Sri Lanka, she grew up in northern Italy, submerged in the wine culture of Piedmont, one of the most respected winemaking regions in the world.

'Wine is part of everyday life there. It's normal for your dad to be growing vines in the garden,' she reminisces. Maheshika studied viticulture and winemaking, travelling the world before finding herself at Tillingham (p.42), a boutique winery in southern England. 'Travelling makes some of the differences you experience as a woman more obvious. The industry isn't always woman friendly. Often it comes down to something physical, like, they assume you can't move as many barrels. And that might be true, but I bring other things.'

'Many things can go wrong in a winery, especially when working with spontaneous fermentation, and without stabilisation... That's why you study.' When I met Maheshika, in the winery at Tillingham in between processes, she was reading a hefty book on enological chemistry (the science of wine). Having made wine in a number of different regions, Maheshika has a broad understanding of how the high acidity and low alcohol produced by grapes grown in England can create challenges. Deeply thoughtful, she applies her accumulated knowledge to these particular British problems, finding ways to balance acidity with the high-alkaline potassium present in grape stems. 'I find the creativity of winemaking in England very stimulating. A blank page. It gives you a lot of freedom.'

For Maheshika, inclusion must reach beyond simply being open to women and people of colour joining the wine industry. 'When we talk about tasting notes, for example, we connect everything to Western food and flavour,' she explains. 'Sometimes I smell the wine and for me it smells of mango lassi. But if I point it out, people don't know what I mean.

'There are people in the industry who are working to make things better. If you have sommeliers and people that talk about wine in a way that actually includes people from every kind of background, that's a way of opening a door to everyone. Wine can be a thing that brings people together.'

The woman behind Scotland's first low-intervention wine fair

The Promoter: India Parry Williams

Once a year, thirsty winemakers and revellers from across the UK and beyond descend upon Edinburgh for a day of tasting and discovery at the Wild Wine Fair, founded in 2017 by Jo Radford – the owner of Timberyard, the ingredient-led restaurant where the fair takes place – and India Parry Williams.

I joined India for an afternoon in Timberyard's courtyard, over a bottle of wine from Tillingham (p.42), to talk about the Wild journey. 'The fair is about getting everyone together in the same room,' she explains, 'connecting people who drink and enjoy wine with people who make it, so that they can taste and talk and learn, and have a laugh.'

India saw the impact of these first-hand conversations early on in her career. 'I was quite young, and you know, being young and female, nobody in the industry paid much attention,' she says, laughing. 'But customers were keen to listen – it was proof that this knowledge doesn't have to come from an older man in red corduroy trousers.'

Bringing both winemakers and wine lovers together in the same space, India had the chance to join the dots between knowledge and discovery on a wider scale. 'I think that's the really cool thing when it comes to talking about English and Welsh wines. The fact that people can go there, visit the vineyard, meet the maker, see the vines – it really helps forge this sense of connection. To me, that's where the strength and growth will be.'

'When I first tasted English sparkling wines, they were a bit of a hard sell – similar to Champagne but not quite Champagne – so I left them alone for a while. And then at a tasting I tried Ancre Hill (p.78), and I was blown away by it. The best English and Welsh wines, for me, come from producers doing things differently, like working with amphora, or skin-contact fermentation.'

'With Edinburgh being a smaller city in a smaller market, it's not always easy when you're trying to specialise in these kinds of craft products, you can't always get hold of things. But then, if you want to do the same as everyone else, the road has already been trodden, it's easy. With Wild we are doing things differently, just like our winemakers. It's harder, but we love it.'

The tastemaker introducing an international audience to new British wine

The Sommelier: Dominic Smith

RIGHT:
Dominic Smith at Luca in Clerkenwell, a fine dining restaurant that serves Italian cuisine using British seasonal ingredients.

Mercury-Award-winning drum and bass producer, rapper and MC, Dominic Smith (aka Dynamite MC) has spent decades at the forefront of British music, collaborating with the industry's biggest names and performing at some of the most renowned clubs in the world. He also happens to be an extremely talented and experienced sommelier who's worked in some of London's most respected and Michelin-starred restaurants, including The Clove Club and Luca, as well as judging one of the largest and most influential wine competitions, the Decanter World Wine Awards.

'Winemakers are creative,' Dominic reflects, 'When they talk about some new bit of equipment in the winery, they'll have sparks in their eyes. Just like my music producer friends when they talk about a new keyboard or a snare. It's a different medium, but it's the same passion.'

Although there is a preconception that the world of wine is stuffy and close-minded, Dominic says that he's mostly found guests to be very willing to experiment with wine. 'I encourage people to try English wine, which is especially exciting for international guests who might not know that we're making great wine here. I'm a massive fan of British wine, particularly sparkling. It's no mystery that we excel, thanks to the similarity of soil types we share with the Champagne region. We're making some sensational sparkling wines, take Nyetimber's Blanc de Blanc (made from 100 percent Chardonnay) – the subtlety of those lovely vanilla notes, the depth from the extended time on the lees. The freshness of acidity that we're achieving with our Chardonnay is world class.'

Dominic is also an admirer of newer wineries at the other end of the spectrum, like Tillingham (p.42) and Westwell (p.118), as well as urban wineries Blackbook (p.54), Renegade (p.140) and London Cru (p.152). 'There are people making amazing wine in these concrete dwellings, in places where you would never expect to find a winery. There are wines that are more effervescent, more charged. You have these wonderful creative labels and you just know that this is a fun, fearless bottle of wine. Then you have wines that are more laid-back and contemplative, more serious. You know, we're a force to be reckoned with.'

The

Wine

The vineyard and winery where ancient methods make modern wines

Tillingham

Dew Farm, in rural East Sussex, is home to a centuries-old oast house, and a cutting-edge way of winemaking. When Ben Walgate founded Tillingham in 2016, he was among the first of a rising movement of winemakers to burst the bubble of traditional-method English sparkling (that is, sparkling wine made according to the labour-intensive, double-fermentation method traditionally used by winemakers in Champagne), and switch up the format with alternative varieties, blends and

methods, quite unlike anything seen before in the UK. Tillingham's distinctive wines turn heads with their graphic labels and boldly coloured liquids – some electric orange, others tinged grape-green with a vitalising shock of acidity. There are wines that stray far from the norm (and might not be for the faint-hearted) and others that are more familiar, but no matter what style of wine they make, they have been a disruptive and creative force – showing what can be done with a touch of imagination.

Having spent six years at Gusbourne, one of the country's most prestigious vineyards, Ben had a clear vision of what he wanted to do when he set up Tillingham. It began not with the wine, but with the soil and regenerative farming: a practice dedicated to replenishing the health of the land and restoring the organic matter stripped away

'Making wine in England, with no real tradition or constraints, means that anything is possible. So why not?'

BEN WALGATE

by decades of industrial farming. Regenerative farming aims to improve soil health while encouraging vibrant polycultures that mimic the diversity of natural ecosystems. The soils at Dew Farm teem with life; wild grasses creep between the different varieties of vines, swaying to a chorus of insects. Further afield, cows chew cud and gaze at Tillingham's many visitors, who are drawn to the vineyard not just for its excellent wines, but also its bucolic surroundings.

The winery is an incubator for creativity. Ben and his winemaking team play with experimental winemaking techniques, many of which are, like the regenerative practices out in the vineyard, rooted in older traditions. For Tillingham's Qvevri Orange wine, grapes such as Bacchus, Müller-Thurgau, Madeleine Angevine and Ortega might be hand-crushed or foot-stomped before fermenting and ageing on skins in qvevri clay pots (otherwise known as amphora) buried in the earth beneath the oast house, so they can ferment underground, according to the millennia-old methods of Georgian winemakers. In general, Ben prefers to work by hand as it allows the winemakers to examine the

LEFT:
The oast house where clay qvevri are buried in the earth. Qvevri are huge amphora, or urns, used for millennia by winemakers in Georgia. Grapes are fermented in the qvevri, which is then sealed, with frequent samples taken to check the progress.

process up-close. 'The gentler we can be throughout a wine's journey,' he explains, 'the better the wine will be. It's like farming, the more in tune we are with the land the better the results will be.'

Tillingham's wines are released in small batches from around 20 different cuvées (or blends) each year; some may be reiterated for several vintages to come, while others are released in tiny quantities, as few as two hundred bottles – a snapshot of a vintage, gone in a flash and perhaps never to be seen again. One such limited release wine was the 2018 Flor, a small batch modelled on the Vin Jaune wines of Jura (a region in France whose winemaking traditions have inspired many contemporary low-intervention producers). Pinot Blanc grapes were pressed and the juice racked into the barrels, where the surface of the liquid, left in contact with a pocket of air, develops a layer of flor yeast. The resulting wine took on the distinctly nutty aroma of those of Vin Jaune wines – rich, almost sweet and utterly moreish.

It is difficult to think of a method that Tillingham hasn't explored, from carbonic maceration (a technique popular in Beaujolais, in which uncrushed grapes ferment whole in their unbroken skins so that very little tannin is extracted and the final juice is fresh, fruity and fun) to trendy pét-nats. Short for *pétillant-naturel* – which means 'natural sparkling' in French – pét-nats are wines made effervescent by being bottled midway through fermentation, so that the resulting carbon dioxide is trapped within the liquid. It's a gentler method of creating sparkling wine than the traditional Champagne style, where an injection of additional sugar and yeast is added to a complete wine to create livelier bubbles. But no matter what

MIDDLE:
Grape skins left over
after pressing are
known as 'pomace'.
This white grape
pomace might be put
into the juice to impart
flavour, colour and
tannins, creating an
orange wine.

BOTTOM:
Ben draws wine from
one of the qvevri. Buried
in the ground, these clay
pots remain at a stable
temperature, allowing
for slow, gradual
fermentation.

> 'The gentler we can be throughout a wine's journey, the better the wine will be. It's like farming, the more in tune we are with the land the better the results will be.'

BEN WALGATE

style they turn their hand to, Tillingham seems to excel at it. As Ben says, 'Farming and making wine in England, with no real tradition or constraints means that anything is possible. So why not?'

British wine tourism is a new industry, yet some vineyards may be guilty of leaning a little heavily on the 'Englishness' of it all, donning tweed and offering guests a glass of sparkling and a scone. All delightful, but Tillingham's on-site restaurant and wine rooms are a reminder that there are other ways to enjoy a glass of English wine. Ben's gentler principles of regenerative farming have rippled through to the kitchen where seasonal, low-waste dishes are assembled from the garden produce and mouthwatering wines are brought up from the cellar. There are worse ways to spend a weekend than waking up in one of their boutique rooms, and enjoying a misty morning ramble across the countryside and through the pretty streets of Rye before heading back to the barn for a wood-fired pizza and a chamomile-and-cardamom-scented glass of orange wine. Tillingham's is a fresh take on tourism and their design-led getaway draws crowds from all over the country.

For Ben, the new wave of British wine has only just begun and there's a long but promising journey ahead. 'It comes from a realisation that conventional farming has to change, and that prescriptive winemaking is dull. I hope I'm wrong but I imagine that the majority of wineries are still pretty conventional, so it's great to see people trying out cool stuff, like Tim Phillips (p.158), Dan Ham (p.196), Adrian Pike (p.118) and Will Davenport (p.68). We're still a minority, but there's hope at least.'

VISIT
Tillingham
Dew Farm
Peasmarsh
East Sussex
TN31 6XD

SOCIAL
@tillinghamwines

WEBSITE
tillingham.com

BOTTLES OF NOTE:

QVEVRI WHITE (PINOT BLANC AND PINOT NOIR), 2021
A pale gold wine with notes of preserved lemon on the nose. Zippy and lithe on the palate, with layers of fruit, as well as earthy notes from the qvevri.

ENDGRAIN (ORTEGA AND AUXERROIS), 2021
Bright with white, green-gold hues. Stone fruit rises from the macerated Ortega, while the Auxerrois brings a crisp acidity in line with this cooler vintage. One of the most laid back and quaffable Endgrains to date.

PINOT NOIR, 2021
A light red with aromas of fresh raspberry and hints of spice, as well as a very light kiss of tannins on the palate. Juicy and gluggable to the last drop.

The radical winery making high-quality wines
on an industrial estate

Blackbook Winery

In the depths of an industrial estate in Battersea, Sergio Verrillo, co-founder of Blackbook Winery, scales the oak barrels stacked high beneath the ceiling of a Victorian railway arch. He reaches a pipette into one of the casks and draws off a little of the brilliant, lemon-hued Pinot Blanc within. The grapes for this batch were hand-picked in Essex a few months ago. In the glass, it's all lime zest and youthful effervescence. The wine is still in its infancy; it will soften over time as it rests in the

barrel, taking on new depths and textures from the oak before eventually being bottled and released.

The small winery is crammed with all sorts of equipment: stainless steel fermentation tanks gleam among the sea of barrels while cages heave with bottles ready to be labelled, a machine already loaded with a ream of block-coloured prints. At the entrance to the arch, forklift trucks rattle by and sirens blare against the rumble of overhead trains – it's all part of inner-city winemaking.

Blackbook Winery was brought to life in 2017 by Sergio and his wife Lynsey, inspired by their love of Chardonnay and Pinot Noir, in particular the taut, mineral whites and silky reds of Burgundy. These well-known grapes just so happen to thrive (when cared for properly) in the British climate. Although in England, Chardonnay and Pinot Noir are typically associated with traditional-method sparkling

'One of the first things people say when they hear about a winery in London is, "What? They have vineyards in London?" But wineries don't need to have their own vineyards, you can make wine on a grungy estate.'

SERGIO VERRILLO, PICTURED LEFT

wines (along with Pinot Meunier), here, they form Blackbook's core range of classic, single-variety still wines made with precise fermentation and generous oak ageing.

Alongside these Chardonnay and Pinot Noir-based core wines, Sergio also experiments with other varieties like Pinot Gris and Sauvignon Blanc. These are more of a challenge to grow in our cool, damp country but can produce outstanding wines, as can the niche-until-now Seyval Blanc, an early-ripening modern hybrid bred for its ability to grow in lower temperatures, whose mouthwatering potential has been overlooked until recently. From this, Sergio crafts an energetic sparkling, with delicate elderflower and a flash of citrus brightness. Regardless of what kind of wine is being made, every single grape is sourced from within two hours' drive of the city.

'One of the first things people say when they hear about a winery in London is, "What? They have vineyards in London?" But wineries don't need to have their own vineyards, you can make wine on a grungy estate,' enthuses Sergio.

LEFT:
Blackbook Winery is filled with old French oak barrels. Most of their vintages are fermented in these barrels as it lends the wine a more rounded texture.

Indeed, urban wineries are a growing phenomenon; one that started in California around 20 years ago and has since spread around the world – from New York to Sydney, Amsterdam and, of course, London. In fact, though the French might well cry *sacrilège*!, even the top of the Eiffel Tower housed a pop-up winery in 2019, several miles from (and a few hundred feet higher than) the nearest vineyards. The concept of sourcing grapes from one region and making the wine in another isn't unique to urban wineries. Throughout France, and just about any other wine region in the world, there are vignerons who grow grapes, and winemakers who, well, make wine. It's good to specialise.

'Essex has a growing number of vineyards,' says Sergio. 'They get lots of sunshine and have this great microclimate. Our Seyval Blanc comes from Yew Tree vineyard in Oxfordshire.' And in 2018, Blackbook collaborated with Forty Hall vineyard (p.108) in Enfield, North London, to make the first 'London-grown, London-made' wine, Tamesis Bacchus (Tamesis being an ancient name for the River Thames).

Sergio came to London from Connecticut ten years ago with dreams of joining a record label and forging a career in the music industry, but instead found himself among the wine teams of some of the city's most renowned fine dining restaurants, including Ottolenghi's Nopi. His past life as a sommelier means Sergio knows a thing or two about how wine should taste. Add a degree in winemaking from Plumpton Agricultural College in Sussex, as well as stints during harvest at respected vineyards around the world, and he also knows how they should be made.

At Blackbook, Sergio combines an appreciation of classic production methods with elements of low-intervention winemaking – like using low-to-no sulphur and indigenous yeasts. Sulphites have been used by winemakers for centuries to stabilise the wine and to prevent oxidation. In small quantities they preserve the fresh flavours of the grapes, but when used heavily they can cause sensitivities like headaches. Forgoing sulphites can lead to wines that are unstable, that may change in the bottle, or develop unpleasant aromas due to faults – but a thorough understanding of winemaking, coupled with plenty of time for the liquid to rest, means it's entirely possible to make high-quality wines without the chemicals. Blackbook's labels may be funky, but the wines themselves are clean.

'We make the kind of wines we like to drink,' says Sergio, 'and we're big on texture – so we love oak for that,' he gestures towards the stack of barrels. 'We'd have a lot more room if we didn't!' The majority of fermentation takes place in French oak and stainless steel tanks, with wines aged on the lees (the liquid spends extra time in contact with spent yeasts leftover from fermentation)

for a minimum of six months, giving the liquid a beautiful sensation of roundness, and that signature smooth texture.

Their Night Jar Pinot Noir Reserve from the core range is a stand-out example. Sourced from Clayhill Vineyard in Essex, this red wine spends 24 months in oak barrel and a further 12 resting in bottle. It's soft and supple, elegant and refined. With dark florals, blackcurrant and warming spice together with velvety tannins, it's unlike anything you might expect from England (where we're better known for producing high-quality sparkling and white wines than reds), let alone a city-centre winery.

On this particularly grey morning, when the clouds seem to mirror the concrete on the ground, I have to ask: why an industrial estate in south London? And not, say, the sun-drenched vineyards of California? 'Oh, dude, we definitely thought about those vineyards,' laughs Sergio. 'But seeing the microbreweries, and then later the urban wineries out there, I guess the idea of doing something in a city was always in the back of our minds in some way. So when it came to exploring our options, we thought, why don't we try to figure out a way to do that here? We really just loved London.'

There are nods to their love of London in the wine labels: the Chardonnay Painter of Light is an ode to London-born artist J. M. W. Turner,

ABOVE:
Sergio and Lynsey Verrillo
founded Blackbook in
2017. Everything from
fermentation to storing
and labelling, as well as
wine tastings, is done on-
site in their small space.

> 'The English wine scene is growing...
> If I'd tried this 25 years ago I'd have
> been laughed out of the city.'

SERGIO VERRILLO

while other bottles depict motifs from the London Transport networks – including historical fonts of the Metropolitan line and tube station tiles from Sergio and Lynsey's commute.

'I'll be totally honest, we set off with the understanding that this project would fail,' Sergio shrugs. 'We're self-funded, setting up a brand-new business in this new way, with English fruit... The odds were stacked against us.' Yet, as Blackbook celebrates its fifth birthday, sales are rising, people are visiting the arches for tastings and critics are full of praise, recently awarding Blackbook's Painter of Light a gold medal at the WineGB Awards.

'The English wine scene is growing, and there's a definite underbelly of people doing these interesting things. If I'd tried this 25 years ago I'd have been laughed out of the city. For us, it's about looking forward, and seeing how we can push these boundaries. We've loved the journey.'

VISIT
Blackbook Winery
Arch 41, Broughton Street
London
SW8 3QR

SOCIAL
@blackbookwinery

WEBSITE
blackbookwinery.com

BOTTLES OF NOTE:

TAMESIS (BACCHUS, FROM FORTY HALL VINEYARD), 2018
Although Sergio was not always a fan of Bacchus as a variety, these organically grown grapes come from a vineyard in north London (p.108) run as a social enterprise. A perfect fit for Blackbook.

PYGMALION (CHARDONNAY, FROM CROUCH VALLEY VINEYARD), 2020
This wine perfectly showcases the longer ageing potential of English Chardonnay. The 2020 vintage was superb, and this wine really does show it.

NIGHTJAR (PINOT NOIR, FROM CLAYHILL VINEYARD), 2020
Nightjar often surprises people by showing how good a red wine from the UK can be. Again, 2020 was an optimal year for it, and the Pinot Noir really shines through in this vintage.

The neighbourhood bottle shop shining a light on local produce

Lola Provisions

It's mid-morning at Lola Provisions and the air is filled with the smell of freshly ground beans and cinnamon buns. Sunlight illuminates the counter loaded with enormous pastries, cured meats and craft beer as a delivery arrives from the local dairy.

The relaxed, slightly nostalgic, atmosphere of this neighbourhood deli and wine bar in Leamington Spa might seem effortless, but it's the culmination of the owners' years of experience gained working at some of the most beloved restaurants in the UK. Founders Katie and James

Jensen (pictured overleaf) met at Hawksmoor over ten years ago. Katie was overseeing the wine list and James was a manager, and in the intervening years both have done stints at Polpo and Soho Farmhouse, all the time forming an idea of what their own space would be like. While they have the skill and knowledge to create a big city-slicker restaurant of their own, they wanted something that would bring them closer to their customers.

'I know it sounds cheesy,' says Katie, 'but we always dreamed of having something a bit like the *Cheers* bar – seeing the same faces and really getting to know our customers. People are very supportive of independent businesses in Leamington Spa. There's a big community here. There's also a good amount of thoughtfulness surrounding food – whether that's to do with

RIGHT:
Co-owner, James Jensen, with British bottles from Offbeat (p.196), Matt Gregory (p.202) and Westwell (p.118).

> '**English wine is worlds away from where it was ten years ago. I think they used to taste quite sharp, but now there is an elegance and gentle acidity.**'

KATIE JENSEN

sustainability, or provenance. We had a feeling that really good quality wine might just work here as well.'

Looking back, Katie admits that she wasn't always that interested in wine: 'When I was nineteen and working in a pub in Hackney, I thought wine was this "middle class, white man" thing. I thought it meant money and dusty bottles of Bordeaux so I wasn't really interested. But then the owner of the pub showed me another completely different side to wine – smaller names, more approachable styles and price points, as well as new regions. It was so fun. The wine was delicious, but it was the people and the culture that felt really exciting.'

Since then, Katie and James have gathered a collection of wines that reflect the values that first sparked her interest: organic, local, sustainable, diverse and accessible.

Just a few country miles away in the Leicestershire Wolds, Matt Gregory (p.202) grows Pinot Noir, Pinot Gris, Solaris, Regent and Bacchus grapes in a tiny plot surrounded by arable farmland.

LEFT:
By offering selected wines on tap, Lola Provisions cuts down on waste. It also reduces the chance of cork taint and requires less storage space than a crate of bottles.

It's the same farmland illustrated on a bottle of Ancestral Red that James lifts from the shelf. It is a sparkling red wine, the liquid fizzing and foaming as it fills the glass, releasing aromas of hedgerow fruits and berries.

'English wine is worlds away from where it was ten years ago,' Katie tells me. 'I think they used to taste quite sharp, but now there is an elegance and gentle acidity. And the reds can have a real finesse!'

The deli is bustling with customers getting coffee or picking up something from the counter for dinner, most stopping to browse the shelves of colourful bottles lining the wall. 'The fun bottles often help of course,' Katie laughs, 'and the low alcohol you commonly get with low-intervention wine is more and more popular. The younger crowd get excited by these wines and are eager to try them. They appreciate the work that goes into the bottle, and accept that the price can be higher. The older generation can take a bit more convincing,' she shrugs, 'but once they've tasted a glass or two, in all honesty there's no going back.'

'Ultimately, we're looking for delicious wine made with the right ethos. We feel really lucky to be part of a community that celebrates British winemakers. Thinking back to that dream of how we wanted the space to feel, there are times when I walk in and there are people there, drinking wine, chatting to James and to each other. I just love it.'

Pioneering organic farmer who's inspired
a generation of emerging winemakers

Davenport Vineyards

Will Davenport is somewhat of an unsung hero in
the world of wine, an integral figure who's helped
shape the landscape of organic winemaking in the
UK over the last two decades. One of the earliest
commercial organic growers, he planted his first
vines in 1991 across just five acres. Now, 20 years
later, Davenport Vineyards has grown to more than
25 acres across five different sites spanning two
counties – Kent and Sussex. But despite running

RIGHT:
Will Davenport, owner
and winemaker, standing
among the vines at
Limney Farm in East
Sussex, near his winery.
Davenport also has a
second, larger vineyard:
Horsmonden in Kent.

his own vineyard and winery, Will has always
made time to share words of wisdom with up-and-
coming organic vineyards when asked. Involved
with Forty Hall (p.108) since its inception, he has
also been a guiding voice to others, but, although
a determined advocate, he is the first to admit that
organic farming isn't easy. 'Many vineyard owners
have been to visit us pre-conversion while they're
deciding whether to go organic or not, and I'm
happy to point out that it's not the right choice
for everyone.'

'A really important aspect of our winemaking
has always been that we can grow the grapes
without using chemicals,' Will says. 'Because
we've been around for a while, we have vineyards
planted with what people might call "old fashioned"
varieties,' he laughs. 'Like Ortega and Faber, which
no one seemed to want anymore.'

'I want to make wines that reflect the grape variety, climate and soil... It would be a shame to mess around with this clean, pure fruit in the winery.'

WILL DAVENPORT

Some of these 'unfashionable' varieties were planted during the first wave of British winemaking in the 1970s, and quite possibly valued more for their resistance to disease and ability to withstand adverse weather than their dazzling flavour. In the decades in between, British winemakers discovered they could grow eminent grapes like Chardonnay, Pinot Noir and Pinot Meunier, and these early workhorse varieties promptly fell out of favour. But, as we all know, things come back around, and some of these long-forgotten grapes are in vogue once again.

Will saw the appeal from the outset, and proved that, in the right hands, these varieties have their allure. 'When we started off in 1991, sparkling wine was a minor part of what was happening in the UK – vineyards were focused on off-dry white wines. I trained in Australia where it's all about keeping sugar levels down and retaining freshness. So here, I could see that the quality of the fruit was just incredible – with high acids that give that desired freshness, as well as being really aromatic. So when we planted our first vineyard, Horsmonden in Kent, we went with all the old-fashioned English varieties, and I love them.'

Davenport's first wine, Horsmonden Dry White, is made up of Ortega, Bacchus, Faber,

Huxelrebe and Siegerrebe. While Faber, for instance, is a fairly neutral white grape that might not wow anyone on its own, in the right blend it can add a flash of brightness and a mouthwatering freshness. Horsmonden is vibrant with lime zest and apple, soft blossom and ripe peach. Refreshing, crisp and easy to drink, it's become something of a cult hit, and has been produced every year since 1993.

From his winery in the old dairy barn on Limney Farm (pictured left), Will crafts a range of styles from nine different varieties. 'Our main focus is on producing the best possible quality grapes; the winemaking can then be left to natural processes in many ways,' Will says. 'I want to make wines that reflect the grape variety, climate and soil because I believe that's the main USP of really good English wines.'

Will has been working for years to reduce the interference of the winemaker, whether that means eliminating additives, like cultured yeasts and fining agents, or avoiding filtration where possible. 'This couldn't happen if we didn't grow superb grapes,' he explains, 'which is why so much effort goes into the vineyard. It would be a shame to mess around with this clean, pure fruit in the winery.'

Organic and low-intervention winemaking methods are crucial to his vision, but so is making a good bottle that everyone can understand and enjoy. 'We're trying to do minimal intervention, while still producing quite a conventional style of wine. Something you could put on the shelf in a supermarket and people wouldn't think it was unfamiliar or weird.'

LEFT:
Davenport combines traditional techniques with the latest equipment. In the winery, oak barrels sit next to stainless steel vats, and there's both a modern pneumatic press and a small basket press.

RIGHT:
Sparkling wines are tested for sulphur, which occurs naturally during fermentation. The winery now uses modern equipment that can analyse multiple samples in a short space of time, but Will studied chemistry at university and occasionally still enjoys doing it the old-school way.

An integral part of the British wine scene since its new beginning, Will has seen the ebb and flow of different styles. While the UK will likely always produce great Champagne-style wines, he thinks that soon winemakers could be turning their attention to red wines made from Pinot Noir, as grapes originally destined for sparkling can be used to make earthy, complex, powerful-yet-poised reds with serious ageing potential – not unlike the revered Burgundy. 'We've always been very adaptable in this country. You know, we spot an opportunity and then someone else tries it and then everyone else thinks, yeah, that's good. I like that.'

VISIT
Davenport Vineyards
Limney Farm
Rotherfield
East Sussex
TN6 3RR

SOCIAL
@limneyfarm

WEBSITE
davenportvineyards.co.uk

BOTTLES OF NOTE:

DIAMOND FIELDS PINOT NOIR, 2020
A red wine with flavours of cherries and blackberry matured in oak barrels. It has a good dark colour and plenty of depth while the solid tannic structure promises that it will become even better with age.

HORSMONDEN DRY WHITE (BACCHUS, ORTEGA, HUXELREBE, FABER AND SIEGERREBE), 2021
A dry aromatic white wine made from grapes grown in Horsmonden in Kent. It has beautiful hedgerow aromas with citrus and peach.

LIMNEY ESTATE BLANC DE BLANCS (CHARDONNAY), 2015
This traditional-method sparkling wine is aged for six years in the bottle. It shows a rich, soft brioche and apple flavours. It is delicious right now but also capable of further ageing.

'We've always been very adaptable in this country. You know, we spot an opportunity and then someone else tries it and then everyone else thinks, yeah, that's good. I like that.'

WILL DAVENPORT

The Canadian sommelier behind a bottle shop
and restaurant that supports sustainable makers

Isca Wines

'I don't know if you've ever tried growing vegetables at home?' Caroline Dubois asks. We're at the table at Isca Wines in Manchester, the wine bar, bottle shop and deli run by sommelier Catherine and chef Isobel Jenkins. Between us sit great slices of sourdough and churned butter, and a bottle of red wine. 'It's really hard,' she laughs. 'It's so much labour for growers and farmers, to get just a little bit of produce. And if they go further

than that and want to be organic or biodynamic, like this?' She lifts her glass and swirls the currant-coloured liquid to demonstrate, 'Then all of that work has to be done by hand. It's mad.'

It's a good point. Growing vegetables is hard, even the smallest allotment takes work, and so when Caroline puts grape-growing into this context, and especially in our marginal, difficult climate, she's right, it does seem a bit mad.

This reverence for the hard work behind good ingredients runs deep through Isca Wines. In the kitchen, Isobel creates home-cooked, rustic dishes from seasonal ingredients supplied by the local growers they work with. The day's menu is scrawled directly onto the glass counter: fresh buns and pillowy quiches, farmhouse cheeses and preserves from neighbouring makers. Meanwhile, Caroline curates a wine selection from her favourite

'Every bottle that I have, there's a reason for it to be here. And the reason for it to be here is that I truly believe that the way these producers are working is improving the way we live. And that's what matters to me.'

CAROLINE DUBOIS

small producers across Europe, so that the floor-to-ceiling shelves are filled with colourful bottles from independent winemakers and artisans, many of whom she knows having spent time in their vineyards.

As a French Canadian, Caroline Dubois first got a taste for natural wine in Montreal: 'It is just the norm there, people don't have to specify "natural" anymore, it's just "wine". But when I moved to Manchester, I couldn't find anywhere that served it. For me, wine is like food. It's fermented grape juice. People are more aware of organic fruit and vegetables, but not so much about what they drink. That is changing.'

Caroline focuses on natural, low-intervention and biodynamic producers who follow sustainable and ethical farming methods. Sourcing wines from the UK means that she can visit the vineyards and get to know the producers on a deeper level.

'When I talk to my customers about wine, it's always about the people behind them,' Caroline explains. 'My intention is never to talk technically. It's to share the stories – the way they are working, living and who they are.'

Caroline pours a glass of Offbeat's (p.196) Field Notes. It is a heady mix of Pinot Noir and Pinot Blanc that tastes like wild cherries and herbs; light in colour, delicate yet complex, with a savoury edge. 'Although some natural wines can be quite funky, the wines from Offbeat are always pretty. The biodynamic farming method Dan Ham follows is very strict, you need to be in full synergy with the environment,' Caroline explains. 'But really, I think, for me, where the magic happens is with his freedom in the cellar. He is focused on watching the wine as it develops, following it to see what it will become, rather than trying to force it into a particular style through heavy-handed winemaking.'

Just as food can be heavily processed, so too can wine. Lab-grown yeast strains can impart certain predictable flavours, as can temperature-controlled fermentation, chaptalisation (the addition of sugar) and excessive filtering and fining. 'Nothing added and nothing taken away' is one way to sum up the minimal intervention ideal.

For Caroline, Isca is not just a place to have an outstanding glass of wine at the end of a long day – it's about something bigger than that: 'Every bottle that I have, there's a reason for it to be here. And the reason for it to be here is that I truly believe that the way these producers are working is improving the way we live. And that's what matters to me.'

Biodynamic vineyard at the forefront of new Welsh wines

Ancre Hill

The mention of vineyards in Wales is often met with surprise, and sometimes with flat-out disbelief. But Ancre Hill, nestled deep in the Monmouthshire hills near the jaw-droppingly beautiful Wye Valley, is one of a steadily growing number of vineyards in Wales. In fact, winemakers from Abergavenny in the south to Powys in the north are quietly proving to be among the most inventive in Britain. They are leading the way with a mix of traditional-method sparkling and still wines made from internationally respected varieties, like Chardonnay and Pinot Noir, as well as from modern, hardy hybrids (grapevines created to have more resistance against disease) that can ripen even in damp and rainy climates. In recent years, wines from these valleys have been pleasing palates on judging panels as well as impressing adventurous wine aficionados on the lookout for something new.

Taking advantage of Wales' northern latitude (which means gloriously long daylight hours in the summer) and a growing interest in new winemaking methods, Ancre Hill produces some of the most highly commended wines in Britain. One of their stand-out vintages in recent years is the crystalline-bright sparkling Blanc de Noir 2010, made from 100 percent Pinot Noir grown in harmony with biodynamic principles that put local wildlife (and quality of the grape, of course) above yields.

Richard Morris and his wife Joy planted the vineyards back in 2006, starting small with just a few hundred vines and eventually growing to 12 hectares, scattering the hills with Chardonnay, Pinot Noir, Albariño and Triomphe. These grapes are all farmed using organic and biodynamic methods (in fact, it's the only certified biodynamic vineyard in Wales) which not only eschew the use

of chemicals and pesticides but also harvest and prune in accordance with the rhythms of the lunar calendar. At the heart of biodynamic farming is a desire to contribute to the health and diversity of the land, rather than diminish it as traditional intensive farming methods tend to do.

Using holistic techniques, which include the use of homemade herbal sprays to encourage strong vines, Ancre Hill makes a range of brilliant traditional-method sparkling and still wines and a couple of wild cards like pét-nat and orange wine. Orange wine is a type of full-bodied, tannic white wine made by leaving the grape skins and seeds in contact with the juice (hence its other name, skin-contact wine) which has been adopted by many small producers as the winemaking method suits low-intervention practices. Intense, subtly spiced, sometimes sour, orange wines have been made for thousands of years in Georgia but have only been adopted by international winemakers in the last 20 years, after a small number of Italian vintners embraced the style.

The hills of Monmouthshire are surprisingly sun-baked and look not unlike those of northern Italy, save for a few giveaways that place us firmly in the British countryside: rolling green fields, a patchwork of hedgerows and ancient oak trees. 'Sunshine hours are good here,' Richard tells me. 'Believe it or not, these slopes are one of the driest parts of the UK.'

The deep loam and limestone soil, flecked with ancient mudstone, is unusually fertile for a vineyard. Growers tend to prefer poor soils, which encourage the vines to dig deep for nutrients to survive and forces them to put out fruit rather than show off an excess of verdant leaves and shoots. Instead, at Ancre Hill, cover crops are planted to provide some healthy competition, stealing enough of the soil's water and minerals that the vines have to concentrate on the essentials: growing strong roots and plenty of grapes. The vineyards thrum with life as the flora and fauna host a hive of activity; insects and nesting birds, wild deer and boar, all enjoying the carefully cultivated wildness.

'Triomphe was the first grape we planted,' says Richard, 'and we planted it without any kind of science.' A robust hybrid that ripens early and has densely coloured grape skins and deep purple juice, Triomphe hails from the cool, high-altitude hills of Alsace on the border between France and Germany. It shows savoury notes of herbs, spices and red berries. At Ancre Hill, they use Triomphe to produce a deep purple sparkling pét-nat that bursts with black cherry and sage.

One of the other wild cards planted in the Welsh hills is the Albariño grape, rarely spotted outside of Spain's Galicia and northern Portugal. At Ancre Hill it basks quite happily in the valleys, where Richard coaxes cinnamon and nectarine-scented orange wine from the sweet-sour fruit.

'The sunshine hours are good here. Believe it or not, these slopes are one of the driest parts of the UK.'

RICHARD MORRIS

LEFT:
Richard Morris walks the grounds of
his vineyard, looking for chamomile
and other botanicals to make herbal
sprays that he'll use to treat the vines,
according to biodynamic methods.

'Again, there's no real science,' he says. 'I was looking for an aromatic variety, and we popped over to Galicia. It does grow well here,' he adds.

Organic from the start, their low-impact ethos continues in the state-of-the-art winery built from natural materials. A living roof replete with long grasses provides a habitat for the local wildlife, while walls made from straw bales help to keep the winery cool and insulated. Inside, pristine tanks are neatly arranged and small-batch fermentations spurred by wild yeasts bubble away inside concrete eggs (which, like clay qvevri, aid the development of texture) before the resulting wines are laid down to rest in oak barrels, where flavours will meld, soften and develop further.

Walking along a meadow path, Richard points out the different flowers they use to make the herbal infusions, also known as 'tisanes', to spray on the vines as a homeopathic booster to strengthen and protect: chamomile, dandelion, fenugreek and willow. Working biodynamically isn't easy – Ancre Hill is the only vineyard in Wales to do so. 'It's not that it's too cold or too damp,' Richard

explains, 'it's the ever-changing weather that's the biggest challenge'. Since converting to biodynamic farming they've noticed smaller bunches of grapes and lower yields, but it does produce much purer fruit. This clarity beams through their wines, whether sparkling or still.

Richard and Joy call their more experimental wines like the pét-nat and the orange wines 'sui generis', which is a Latin phrase meaning 'unique'. With its combination of Welsh hills, surprising sunshine, wild meadows and biodynamic ethos, Ancre Hill is 'sui generis' indeed.

VISIT
Ancre Hill Estates
Monmouth
NP25 5HS
Wales

SOCIAL
@ancrehill

WEBSITE
ancrehillestates.co.uk

BOTTLE OF NOTE:

ORANGE WINE (ALBARIÑO), 2020
A savoury skin-contact wine with notes of bruised apple. The grapes were hand-harvested and macerated in whole bunches before pressing. The juice was then aged for 10 months in oak barrels.

RIGHT:
Wildflowers grow freely and cover crops are planted among the vines, promoting biodiversity and increasing competition, encouraging them to grow strong roots.

Small-batch English sparkling from Hampshire's famous chalk valleys

Black Chalk

Southern England's chalk soils are to grapes what salt and vinegar is to chips. Enhancing flavour and adding a streak of acidity, chalk helps to create sparkling wines that rival the best produced in France. In fact, the alkaline chalk soils of Hampshire, Kent and Sussex are the same as those that run through Champagne, continuing uninterrupted beneath the Channel, stretching out across the two nations. They provide the perfect conditions for making outstanding wine,

RIGHT:
Jacob Leadley, founder, (pictured left) with assistant winemaker Zoë Driver and viticulturalist James Matyear.

as Jacob Leadley, the winemaker behind the Hampshire-based vineyard Black Chalk, knows very well.

At Black Chalk, Jacob crafts elegant and vivacious wines in the picturesque Test Valley. He works closely with his tight-knit team, which includes assistant winemaker Zoë Driver and viticulturist James Matyear, to produce small-batch, high-quality sparkling and still wines from grapes grown across three small, distinct vineyards on the sprawling estate.

Jacob, Zoë and James have worked in larger vineyards around the world, in Australia, France and New Zealand. Coincidentally, all three have worked, at different points, for Hattingley Valley, a well-respected winery in Hampshire which is responsible for producing upwards of half a million bottles per year.

TOP:
Jacob Leadley and
Zoë Driver inside the
state-of-the-art winery.
Stainless steel tanks,
unlike oak, do not alter
the flavour of the wine
or allow any oxygen to
interact with the juice,
producing a fresh and
fruity vintage.

'Coming from a bigger winery you don't always see everything that's going on,' says Zoë. 'You see only the vineyard or only the winery. At Black Chalk, we're more connected to each other's roles.' Zoë and James have now found their niche working within Jacob's more boutique model, and the chemistry that comes with working in a smaller team is obvious. As we walk through the vineyard the trio joke and jest, in between pointing out the geographical wonders that make Black Chalk such an ideal spot for growing grapes destined for beautiful wines.

Glimpses of flint blocks glisten in the soil, while the chalk bedrock lies far beneath the surface. 'It's the chalk that gives that purity of fruit, that mineral edge,' explains Jacob. 'It prevents anything from compromising the aromas. With Chardonnay in particular you get this 'backbone' that I don't think you get anywhere else on any other soil.'

There are three small, separate vineyards at Black Chalk, named Rivers, The Levels and Hide. 'All three are above chalk, but they also each have their own unique conditions which gives a nice variation. Hide is a real suntrap thanks to the valley, the grapes bask in the warmth here. With conditions like this you can make standalone wines with grapes from just one vineyard that really shout of their specific area.'

Single vineyard wines like the one Jacob describes are only made using grapes from the best sites, when the conditions provide everything the vines could possibly need. The commonly used alternative is to blend grapes from across different sites, getting, for example, grapes with intense concentration of flavour from one, and freshness or minerality from another. The different conditions are expressed through the wine – a concept known as 'terroir': 'The chalk soils and the sunshine come together to give purity of fruit and precision,' Jacob adds, 'if you've got that tension, you can make an absolute blinder of a wine.'

The Hide Single Vineyard wine in question is their newest release: lithe, steely and powerful. It joins a small range which includes a small-batch traditional-method sparkling, a plump and voluptuous sparkling Wild Rosé resplendent with notes of red berries and an elegant, light Dancer in Pink still rosé.

There are still challenges that come with producing wine in England. The growing season is long, as the fruit needs as much time on the vines as possible to ripen in our cooler climes. Although vines will start to bud in early spring, sometimes it's not possible to harvest them until October, and the season has even been known to stretch into November. In the meantime, there can be a lot of poor weather and adverse conditions that winemakers have to contend with.

'Frost in spring, flowering issues, disease, rainy harvest season, splitting grapes,' James says, listing just a few of the difficulties they come up against. I can't help wonder out loud, why anyone would try to make wine in Britain? You'd have to be mad. Jacob agrees, 'It's as much about the people involved and their passion. As you rightly say, you've got to be mad. And to be mad is part of the delight.'

VISIT
Black Chalk Vineyard and Winery
Fullerton Road
Andover
Hampshire
SP11 7JX

SOCIAL
@blackchalkwine

WEBSITE
blackchalkwine.co.uk

BOTTLES OF NOTE:

BLACK CHALK WILD ROSÉ (CHARDONNAY, PINOT NOIR AND PINOT MEUNIER), 2016
A delicate pink colour, the nose is a heady mix of redcurrants with hints of apple. Crisp freshness, creamy texture and an abundance of fruit which lingers on the palate.

BLACK CHALK CLASSIC (CHARDONNAY, PINOT NOIR AND PINOT MEUNIER), 2016
The perfect balance of fruit, weight and freshness. A delicate weight from the Pinot Meunier and beautiful floral aromas from the Chardonnay and Pinot Noir.

The lively bar and bottle shop pairing British wines with seasonal Scottish ingredients

Spry Wines

With its white walls, mid-century modern furniture and pared back aesthetic, Spry might embrace Scandi-chic over traditional tartan touches, but their menu is a real love letter to Scottish ingredients. Whether it's langoustine from Fife or gorse flowers foraged from Edinburgh's green spaces, the dishes are an ever-changing carousel of the seasons.

Owners Matt and Marzena are interested in ingredients that can shine despite the confines of the small kitchen – which stands like an island in the centre of the room, surrounded by low lounge seating. 'We're limited in space, so produce is very important to us,' Marzena explains, referring to their need for high-quality ingredients which require very little to turn into something truly delicious. 'We try to focus on produce from the British Isles because then the quality speaks for itself, and we don't have to do so much to it.' This approach also informs how Matt makes his selection of what wines to pour by the glass, and considers what flavours might come together. 'It's a well-known thing,' Marzena adds, 'What grows together, goes together.'

The couple wanted to create a casual and accessible space where people could hang out and discover low-intervention wines made by small producers. Matt handpicks a selection of wines from all around the world, along with a carefully

'The great thing about working with British winemakers is that they can come to see us, and we can go there.'

MATT JACKSON

curated selection produced in the UK. 'The great thing about working with British winemakers is that they can come to see us, and we can go there. We've been so impressed with the vineyards we've visited.'

Having producers come to the space helps to lessen the distance between those drinking the wine, and those making it. Equally, by having British wines on the shelves from vineyards Matt and Marzena have been to, they're able to share their stories first-hand.

Matt pours a glass of Westwell's Ortega Skin Contact from Kent (p.118), an orange wine that is

LEFT:
A bottle of Tillingham's (p.42) Saw Pit Pinor Meunier from a single plot on the estate. One of the first wines made from grapes grown at Tillingham.

a favourite at Spry. 'We really like this producer – fairly clean in their winemaking, using grapes from their own vineyards and working towards organic farming, which in the UK is super impressive.' The wine is ripe with notes of baked apricot and cinnamon, and a lingering saline dryness. It pairs perfectly with the Cashel Blue cheese on toast with acacia honey and walnuts that Marzena rustles up from the kitchen.

The name, Spry, means lively and energetic – and the wine bar is a hub of activity, as Marzena busily chops and preps a flurry of seasonal plates while Matt circulates with the bottles he's chosen to open on that day. The couple have found creativity in the limits of their space, as well as the hyper-seasonality of their menu. Perhaps the same can be said of British winemakers too, that it is the constraints they encounter – the unpredictable weather, the nascent and still-developing wine scene – that push them to become ever more creative.

Old hop farm converted into the UK's largest organic vineyard

Oxney Organic

Oxney's winery occupies a Grade II-listed oast house, once used to dry hops from the surrounding farm to make beer. That farm, lying in the medieval landscape of High Weald, long admired for its undulating hills and ancient woodlands, is now a vineyard. Oxney is one of the leading (and largest) organic vineyards in the country with 35 acres of lush, sloping vineyards overlooked by a Jacobean farmhouse and a scattering of shepherd huts where guests can stay and sleep off an afternoon spent tasting stand-out sparklings, like the Oxney Organic Estate NV, which has all the

RIGHT:
The Jacobean farmhouse is now a bar, while guests can stay in the shepherd's hut overlooking the vines.

mouthwatering freshness of the first bite of an apple as well as notes of elderflower and pear.

When Kristin Syltevik started the vineyard at Oxney Estate, she knew it had to be sustainable. 'I would not have done it if we couldn't be organic,' she says. 'Agriculture, and therefore viticulture, is one of the worst sinners behind global warming.' Born in Norway, Kristin left a high-flying career in PR for muddy boots and early mornings on the vineyard with her partner Paul Dobson. Together, they have an ecological perspective on grape growing. Kristin talks of the importance of nurturing the fruit: Chardonnay, Pinot Noir, Pinot Meunier and Seyval Blanc grapes bask in the sun (and, quite often, glisten under the rain), before being treated with low-intervention processes in the winery, with minimal sulphites and no filtration. The grapes are sheltered by an oak forest that buffers most of the

> '**Why not have it all? Growers across the world are turning organic or biodynamic because they want to grow the best fruit... our fruit is tastier as we don't kill the terroir.**'

KRISTIN SYLTEVIK

strong winds coming in from the sea, allowing only a gentle breeze to pass through the vines and keep the mildew at bay.

As the largest organic producer in the UK, Oxney proves that it is possible to make top quality, traditional wines, organically, and at volume. As Kristen says, 'Why not have it all? Growers across the world are turning organic or biodynamic because they want to grow the best fruit. We started our organic journey because we are very aware of the environmental impact conventional growing has, but the added benefit is that our fruit is tastier than the average vineyard, as we don't kill the terroir...' Although conventional farming leads to larger and more reliable yields, it can also impact on the flavour and quality of the grape.

Even in Sussex, fast becoming England's most reliable and prestigious wine region, vignerons like Kristin face serious challenges. 'The summer of 2021 was difficult. We lost a lot of fruit due to disease, but then again so did the conventional vineyards. You have to be prepared that, in bad years, you will be lower on yield.'

But even when yields are low, the wines they make are complex, varied and often exceptional. Without pesticides or chemical fertilisers, the vines depend on the earth and climate, growing in tune with the ecosystem that surrounds them. From Oxney's vibrant sparklings to elegant rosés – all rosehips and raspberries – every glass seems to capture the charm of their profoundly English location.

VISIT
Oxney Organic Estate
Beckley
Rye
East Sussex
TN31 6TU

SOCIAL
@oxneyorganicestate

WEBSITE
oxneyestate.com

BOTTLES OF NOTE:

PINOT NOIR, 2020
Intense ruby colour with a complex nose of ripe flavours: tobacco leaf, dried plums, walnuts, dark chocolate and spicy black peppercorns.

CLASSIC (CHARDONNAY, PINOT NOIR AND PINOT MEUNIER), 2018
The dominant grape in this blend is Pinot Meunier, which provides body and richness to the blend. Ripe apple is balanced with freshness and toasty autolytic notes. The soft, generous mouthfeel is pure Oxney.

CHARDONNAY, 2020
Lovely example of a cool climate Chardonnay. The nose has complex aromas of stone fruits and hazelnut, while on the palate some richness comes through with a creamy mouthfeel supported by a backbone of acidity.

Kristin Syltevik worked in PR until a trip to Bordeaux inspired her to consider a career in wine. She started Oxney by planting over 6000 vines by hand.

East London's iconic all-in-one bottle shop,
wine bar and restaurant

P. Franco

Stepping into P. Franco on a Friday night feels a lot like walking into a great house party. Crowds mill around the edges of the room or cosy up on benches by the window, while friends and strangers sit together at the large communal table. Except, unlike most house parties, no one's drinking warm lager and supermarket vodka mixers. P. Franco serves natural, low-intervention wine from independent makers – glasses flow with chilled reds and cloudy whites, some frothing with bubbles – alongside a daily changing menu cooked up on just two induction hobs.

It's a long way from the wine bars of previous decades, when mahogany-panelled rooms with condescending sommeliers and impenetrable wine lists catered to men of a certain age. Instead, P. Franco was inspired by the part-shop, part-bar 'Cave à Mangers' of Paris which serve high-quality wines you can either take away with you or enjoy in situ with charcuterie and other small bites.

'A shop is less intimidating than a wine bar,' Paris Barghchi, who heads up operations, tells me. 'It's about the conversation, and finding a less intimidating way to talk about it all. People are afraid to say the wrong thing, but there is no wrong thing.'

It's certainly more convivial than a traditional wine bar. P. Franco landed on east London's Lower Clapton Road in 2014 – one of the first in the revolution sweeping the British wine scene, disrupting the old formula by welcoming a new generation and less traditional demographic – with compact, curated wine lists and an erudite but approachable style. The team also has a knack for spotting gastronomical talent; some of the country's top chefs have taken up a guest spot

104

IBRAHIM
OMBRA
GUEST CHEF
10-12 DEC

P×F

MANGAL II
Seb
Myers
SUNDAY
01—11—20

PFRAN
NEW
KILN

P×F

JAMIE
SMART
(FLOR)

P×Franco

P.FRANCO

CHASE
LOVECKY

SEPT 19

PFRAN-
CO
CHEF
CHASE
LOV-
ECKY
MAY 19

P×Franco

May 19 / P.Franco's New Resident Chef / Chase Lovecky

F

18
W
D
N

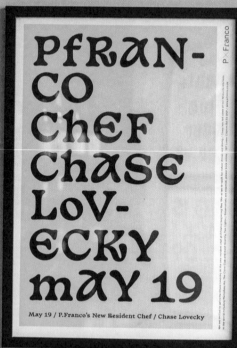

INES

ING

IO ENTRY

SEIS 4RA

Celebrate Emilia-Romagna
With winemaker Federico of Orsi Vigneto San Vito

morta
della
party

STOCKHOLM, Cafe Nizza

COPENHAGEN, Rud

Celebrate
emilia-romagna
with winemaker Federico and Roberto

mortadella party
sunday 10th may
5:30pm at P.franco

dinner
monday 11th may
7:30pm at Brawn

aperitivo
Tuesday 12th may
5 till 7
at Duck Soup

YOTO WINES PRESENTS

CELEBRATE Emilia-Romagna

MORTA
DELLA
PARTY

with winemaker FEDERICO
of ORSI Vigneto San Vito

BRIGHT, 1 Westgate Street E8 3RL

T
NCO

OMBIA

17

23/01

P×Franco

anna
tobias

27

P×Franco

P×Franco

'It's about the conversation, and finding a less intimidating way to talk about it all. People are afraid to say the wrong thing, but there is no wrong thing.'

PARIS BARGHCHI

behind P. Franco's famed hobs, including Kiln's Meedu Saad and Burro e Salvia's Mitchell Damota.

Around the room, shelves are stacked with bottles, an eclectic selection from small producers across the world, with a couple from closer to home. Just like the chefs, the wines poured here often go on to great acclaim. P. Franco has been pivotal in shaping the wine landscape of London and beyond, so to spy new British wines on their shelves is a sure sign of what's to come.

But to land a spot on their shelves, winemakers need to align with P. Franco's ethos of supporting growers driven by respect for the land, farming for healthy grapes and a low-intervention approach in the winery. 'We're looking for producers who don't make wine, they follow the wine,' Paris explains. Traditionally this has led them to the most purist of

natural makers from Jura, Loire, Alsace, Burgundy and the Rhône.

'We've never set out to list English wines just because they're English,' Paris tells me, as we turn to a recent addition to the shelves from Wiltshire. 'Daniel Ham at Offbeat (p.196) is one of those makers who very much watches and listens.'

Offbeat's Watchtower, an organic Pinot Noir and Pinot Meunier sourced from vineyards in Hampshire and Devon, is aged in amphora. Pouring the peach and copper liquid into a glass, Paris is appreciative of Daniel Ham's work. Having lent a hand during harvest at Offbeat, she speaks about their method from direct experience: 'He uses intuition and his understanding of chemistry and biology to influence his decisions... It produces a wine that is really pure, really lively.'

As Will Gee, the bar's General Manager, says, 'It's the agricultural side of things I appreciate. Looking back at France and Italy in the 1970s, there's a purity that winemakers were sort of striving towards then and I think we're starting to see that here. It feels like we are watching something unfold.'

LEFT:
Posters line the walls at P. Franco, designed by Tegan Hendel. Many of the posters celebrate past and present guest chefs.

The capital's only commercial vineyard in over 500 years

Forty Hall Vineyard

'You're having me on,' laughs my Uber driver. 'I've lived in Enfield all my life, and you're telling me there's a vineyard? Here? I don't believe you.'

Admittedly, taking an Uber to a vineyard is a new one for me too, but since 2009 Forty Hall has been growing wine-worthy grapes just inside the M25. There are small commercial vineyards hidden in major cities around the world, including Paris and New York, but Forty Hall is the only commercial urban vineyard in London. Once, our capital had many vineyards used by medieval monasteries and great cathedrals to make wine for Communion. As we pull up beside the 17th-century Grade II-listed barns of the estate, the driver raises an eyebrow, a little sceptical, and asks, 'Is the wine any good?'

I was here to find out. Forty Hall is a ten-acre organic vineyard and community-focused

social enterprise founded by viticulturalist Sarah Vaughan-Roberts in partnership with the environmental college Capel Manor, who generously provided the land. In the last decade Forty Hall has challenged expectations of urban vineyards with wines like its award-winning London Brut Sparkling, the pale gold of an autumn sunrise, with its exuberant bubbles and hints of lemon zest and baked pear.

Part of a working farm, Forty Hall is a constant thrum of activity, even at sunrise. As we arrive, a ginger pig roots and snuffles gleefully through the yard. 'I see you've met Wilma, the family pet,' laughs Emma Lundie, Forty Hall's Head of Operations, as she strides towards me with muddy wellies and a broad grin. 'She's a bit of a celebrity around here.'

This lively barnyard plays host to a farmer's market each month – a taste of village life for weary

Londoners – but on this crisp October morning, we're here for harvest. A short stomp brings us to Warren Field and Long Field, where, lit by the low morning rays, rows of vines wait: Chardonnay, Pinot Noir and Pinot Meunier for the sparkling; Bacchus and Ortega for the still. From the hilltop, two Brutalist tower blocks rise above the foliage, a reminder of the vineyard's unique proximity to the city. On a clear day, we're told you can see The Shard.

Emma briefs a team of volunteers with instructions for the day of picking ahead, interspersed with cheery greetings of 'Morning!' as newcomers arrive. Emma oversees both the running of the vineyard and The Flourish Project – a thriving ecotherapy initiative that aims to boost general well-being of local volunteers through connection with nature and the great outdoors. No mean feat. 'It is a challenge, getting that balance,' admits Emma. 'We want the absolute highest possible quality of grapes, and to give the best volunteering experience. It's important to us that we do both really well.'

And as for the other obvious challenge here, of growing grapes in London, and doing it organically? 'When Sarah planted the vines, everyone said she was mad!' Emma tells me. But Sarah had studied viticulture at Plumpton Agricultural College, just like many of the UK's rising stars including Daniel Ham at Offbeat (p.196) and Sergio Verrillo at Blackbook Winery (p.54). She saw potential in the clay and flint-flecked fields, noticing how they caught just the right amount of sun, and had both a vision – seriously good wine – and an accomplice in the pioneering organic winemaker Will Davenport (p.68).

Some of the volunteers have been coming here for years – or rather, for several harvests, as they measure things around these parts – and are extremely knowledgeable. They move in formation through the verdant corridors, selecting grapes with military precision.

This particular harvest marks the close of the 2021 vintage, a tough one for growers across the country, ravaged by late spring frosts and a summer that languished under grey skies and endless rain. For larger vineyards following more industrial practices, they can just about scrape through a bad year, but for a small, organic business like Forty Hall, it can be devastating. Much of the crop has been lost and there will be no wine made commercially this year, yet this adversity is all part and parcel of training grapes in our marginal climate. Despite everything, the mood is chipper and the team crack jokes as they work. Perhaps it's a British thing.

> ## 'Nature is cyclical. There are good years and bad, but neither one lasts forever.'
>
> EMMA LUNDIE, PICTURED RIGHT

We meet Adam, busy selecting Ortega grapes. He's studying at Capel Manor College and likes the idea of winemaking as a future career. I ask whether this lost vintage has put him off at all: 'If pruning in December didn't put me off, nothing will,' he chuckles. As he speaks, lime green, chattering parakeets swoop and dive from the trees. 'They know when the grapes are ready before we do,' Adam says. While there may not be much in the way of wine grapes on the day I visit, it's still a banquet for the birds.

In a good year, like the outstanding 2018 vintage (and, mercifully, the 2022 vintage that followed the lost year I visited) grapes flourish on the vines, swelling until plump and near-bursting with flavour, before being plucked and sent to Will Davenport's winery in Sussex. His expert hand guides them through a 'minimal intervention' approach that involves little in the way of technical input, and transforms them into wines like the elegant and poised Bacchus, pure and clean with English pear and white flower, or the richer, riper Ortega, all baked apple and quince with a playful finish.

As for this year, the team will pick and press the grapes on site, to make a batch just big enough for them to toast 2021's hard work, and then they'll set about laying the foundations for next year. 'Nature is cyclical,' muses Emma. 'There are good years and bad, but neither one lasts forever.' There's a life lesson in there somewhere.

But to answer my Uber driver – yes, the wine is very, very good.

VISIT
Forty Hall Vineyard
Forty Hall Farm
Enfield
London
EN2 9HA

SOCIAL
@fhvlondon

WEBSITE
fortyhallvineyard.com

BOTTLE OF NOTE:

2019 LONDON BRUT, (CHARDONNAY, PINOT NOIR AND PINOT MEUNIER)
London Brut is Forty Hall's most iconic London wine – a traditional-method sparkling wine, bursting with zestiness and ripe orchard apples. It's ideal as an aperitif.

ABOVE:
White grape skins
remain after pressing,
also known as 'pomace'.
Pomace can be used
to make brandies like
grappa, but it also
makes a fantastic
fertiliser.

Bar and bottle shop revitilising wine for a new generation

Top Cuvée

A cuvée is essentially the French word for a specific batch, barrel or blend of wine, but it's often used to denote a special, particularly high-quality, high-value batch. While the name 'Top Cuvée' may seem like a tongue-in-cheek takedown of the self-seriousness of the wine scene, it is actually an affectionate reference to Brodie Meah's introduction to wine through working in a Michelin-starred restaurant.

'Watching the sommeliers in that kind of environment, they were amazing, and very talented. But also quite intimidating. When pouring the really high-end wines, they'd say "This is the top cuvée of this, the top cuvée of that." It basically meant, it's exclusive and not for everyone.'

'Going to a wine bar doesn't have to be an educational experience,' shrugs Brodie, leaning against the shopfront of Cave Cuvée, the wine shop and bar on east London's siren-soundtracked Bethnal Green Road that is the newer, sister site to the original bar and restaurant, Top Cuvée in Highbury. 'Sometimes you just want to have a glass of wine.' It's a refreshing sentiment. The wine world can be guilty of putting its bottles on a pedestal. And yet Brodie, his business partner Max Venning and their team might be more responsible for the next generation's interest in wine than he's giving himself credit for.

'Anything we can do to make the wine scene more welcoming – we want to do that.'

BRODIE MEAH

Ever since Top Cuvée, the group's flagship restaurant and bar, burst onto the scene in 2019 it's been a runaway success. A few short years since then, with the additions of their online store Shop Cuvée and now Cave Cuvée, they've continued to shake things up with their rebellious selection of bottles from smaller producers communicated to the masses through an irreverent social media presence, as well as their relaxed and informal style of service. Wines from under-the-radar regions like Austria's Carnuntum and England's Kent might be served alongside loaded hotdogs in the subterranean wine bar, or delicately flavoured European small plates like saucisson séche, or lardo, figs and honey.

Brodie wanted to bring the quality ingredients and attention to detail he experienced at top restaurants to something much more casual. 'I wanted a neighbourhood vibe,' as he puts it. 'Taking the sentiment of "top cuvée" but with a relaxed, cartoon-style branding is our way of saying that we work with top-quality ingredients, but we're still approachable.'

With its collision of cheerful design, natural wines and a penchant for slang (where 'wine' becomes 'juice', and easy-drinking styles are described as 'smashable', instead of the more traditional 'quaffable'), Top Cuvée might seem like the epitome of hipster wine culture – and therefore easy for some to sneer at – but no one can deny their success. Both venues are routinely booked up and bottles fly off the shelves. Top Cuvée is helping more people become passionate about wine, especially a younger generation.

'Anything we can do to make the wine scene more welcoming – we want to do that.' Brodie explains, 'Of course, we take the product seriously once you're in here. But when it comes to telling people why these wines are so good, we try to keep it pretty light, to do that in a way that's super approachable as well.'

Events play a key part in introducing wine to new crowds, and the Cave Cuvée basement has hosted supper clubs, winemaker dinners and pouring parties with a variety of themes. The team from Tillingham (p.42) in Sussex has been one of many to pop bottles here, including for the launch of one wine made collaboratively for Top Cuvée: the Tillingham SC20 made with the Champagne trio of Pinot Noir, Pinot Meunier, and Chardonnay and, curiously, a blend of apples. It's bright and crisp, while still being nicely rounded with fruit, and has an indulgent aroma of apple crumble. 'My first experience of English wines was with the bigger stuff, the more high-end sparkling – it was very classic,' Brodie says. 'But now what I rate the most is the modern contemporary style. That said, I think it's cool to have these two different stories, there's space for both.'

Swinging by Cave Cuvée on a Friday evening, the energy is palpable. Customers drop in one after the other to fill up their bright orange tote bags with bottles of gluggable wine. Some stop to chat with the team, asking questions about producers and regions, whether a wine is barrel-aged or skin-contact, and what might work with the dish they're cooking tonight. 'Our whole thing is to introduce people who would otherwise be intimidated. When we get people coming in for the first time who are nervous, and then we see them go on to become wine lovers, it's awesome.'

The man bringing music industry savvy to the British wine scene

Westwell

Adrian Pike's path into winemaking was unconventional. The ex-music industry director co-founded Moshi Moshi Records in the late 1990s – the independent label that brought Florence and the Machine, Bloc Party and Hot Chip to our attention. But after many years of late nights and smoky basements, Adrian and his wife Galia found themselves craving fresh air and a different kind of creativity. So, he retrained and swapped recording studios for rolling hills and, crucially, vineyards.

RIGHT:
A bottle of Westwell Ortega Amphora with a label illustrated by co-founder Galia Pike. She draws inspiration from the vineyard, from fermenting grapes to the fossil-rich soil. Galia explains, 'We wanted the labels to catch the eye in the same way that album artwork does.'

Although initially bound for France to start over as a winemaker, a glass of English wine stopped Adrian in his tracks. 'The pivotal moment was tasting Will Davenport's Horsmonden Dry White (p.68),' he explains. Produced in Kent, the wine is a vibrant blend of Bacchus, Ortega, Faber, Siegerrebe and Huxelrebe grapes, part fermented in huge foudre oak casks (which can hold ten or even twenty times more liquid than a classic barrel, so that less of the surface area of the wine is in contact with the oak) to soften the blend of high-acid varietals and make the wine more textured. It had a complexity and depth to it that was new to Adrian. 'I was amazed it was possible to make wine like that in the UK. A switch flipped and I made the decision then and there that I wanted to make wine in England. I called Will up the next day and began working with him.'

'The UK wine industry is an emerging industry, and yet it's working with something which has its roots deep in history – just like music. It's hard not to be incredibly enthusiastic about making wine here.'

ADRIAN PIKE, PICTURED LEFT

In 2017 he set up Westwell with his wife Galia on the chalk slopes of Pilgrims' Way in the North Downs. They now make an incredibly creative and drinkable range of wines, including some amphora-aged wild ferments. Most winemakers today use cultured yeasts to control fermentation and achieve a desired flavour or aroma but wild fermentation is kicked off by the natural yeasts already in the atmosphere (or on the grape skins). It is riskier and can result in unexpected flavours (some wonderful... others not so wonderful), but it's a method favoured by low-intervention winemakers, as it means fewer additives, and in the right hands wild fermentation can produce complex wines, like Westwell's popular Ortega Skin Contact.

Adrian makes his wine from five grape varieties all grown on site: Pinot Meunier, Pinot Noir, Chardonnay and Ortega, along with a little sprinkling of Rondo. In total, Westwell now has 34 acres under vine and over 50,000 vines. 'In terms of style, we wanted to make wine that was inherently English – wine which accurately reflects our terroir. We work with the grape varieties that really channel the land we're on.'

Westwell is an experimental and innovative winemaker. Although each wine they produce is different, they are all connected by the vineyard's position on the Pilgrims' Way, with its a unique mixture of six different soil types, including sand, clay and chalk, rich with fossils from a time when the entire area lay underwater. They embrace these distinct micro-geologies in their planting: Chardonnay vines are situated on fields with shallower, chalky soils that catch the evening sun; the Pinots are best cultivated in a mix of sand and chalk, while the Ortega is planted in the sandiest, most sheltered spot of all to allow it to develop its distinctively aromatic notes.

'As we progress,' Adrian adds, 'we are trying to manage the land and our production more sustainably – trying to find ways to break the monoculture of conventional viticulture. We want to produce wines with as little intervention as possible that make the most of the grapes we're producing.'

Rather than prescribe a style, Adrian prefers to see what each vintage brings, making the wines best suited to the grapes. Depending on whether a heatwave has boosted sugar levels, or cool nights have provided a flash of acid-brightness, the grapes might become a rose and rhubarb flavoured Westwell Pink or a light red like Summer Field. They could find their way into a spritzy pét-nat or an amber-tinted still wine if they call to be left in contact with skins after pressing (the method by which orange wine is made, as the skins impart

> 'In general, we make wines to be drunk and enjoyed. Wine brings people together, and we always have that in mind when we're producing each harvest.'

ADRIAN PIKE

colour and tannins to what would otherwise be a white wine, giving the liquid not only a deeper hue but also a fuller body). But invariably, it is always the style that best reflects the fruit.

'We want to make really drinkable wines – that's key for us,' Adrian says. 'Some of our wines are more contemplative, such as the Ortega Skin Contact, but in general, we make wines to be drunk and enjoyed. Wine brings people together, and we always have that in mind when we're producing each harvest.'

When Adrian and Galia talk about the wine scene in Britain today, it's clear that they're excited about the years to come. 'I remember having the realisation that our climate was perfect for skin-contact wines, pét-nats and light reds as well as traditional method sparkling. Right now is a pivotal time. Coming here from the music industry, I was also there during one of these seismic shifts. Things were constantly shifting and changing. All of this feels relevant as the UK wine industry is an emerging industry, and yet it's working with something which has its roots deep in history – just like music. It's hard not to be incredibly enthusiastic about making wine here.'

VISIT
Westwell Wine Estates
Charing
Ashford
Kent
TN27 0BW

SOCIAL
@westwellwines

WEBSITE
westwellwines.com

BOTTLES OF NOTE:

PELEGRIM NV (CHARDONNAY, PINOT NOIR AND PINOT MEUNIER)
This classic non-vintage sparkler is a great representation of what Westwell grows, and a real crowd pleaser. It's a fruit-forward wine with red apple flavours, aged for three years on lees for a rich creaminess.

ORTEGA SKIN CONTACT, 2020
Ortega is Westwell's signature grape. It grows brilliantly in England, and is exceptionally versatile with great flavours. Fermented with wild yeast on skins, this golden-orange wine has fantastic depth and texture.

Well-curated bottle shop and bar from the founders of London's favourite beer hotspot

Gnarly Vines

While co-founders Tom McKim and William Jack may have spent their early careers heaving barrels in winery cellars and selling wine on shopfloors, it's beer that they're best known for now. In 2013, they founded Clapton Craft, a small shop in Hackney packed full of pale ales, session beers and fruited sours from independent breweries (many in London) making something much more interesting than the sterilised lager on tap at most pubs. In the last ten years, they have

RIGHT:
A selection of British bottles from wineries like Tillingham (p.42) and Davenport (p.68) have earned their place alongside international wines with a cult following.

opened seven more shops across London as well as a popular subscription service. Now they're bringing that same entrepreneurial energy to the world of wine, offering a platform to small-batch, sustainable wineries and finding them a whole host of new customers who want to know more about the provenance of their bottles and support independent makers. One day, low-intervention wines could be as popular and well known as Five Points or Beavertown – two stand-out London-based breweries.

Gnarly Vines is a relaxed space in Walthamstow with floor-to-ceiling shelves of cult wines from around the world, but specialises in the kind of poised and ethereal styles most famously found in Jura and the Savoie, two alpine regions near the Swiss border in France. Tom and William have curated a collection of bottles

'The first wave of British wine, back around the 1960s, was all about the hybrid varieties. The idea around quality was: if it grows, that's good enough.'

TOM MCKIM

which showcase their admiration for those regions' adventurous winemakers, but nowadays they also have a collection dedicated to English wines. The fact that Gnarly Vines encourages their customers to explore our homegrown vineyards and avant-garde wineries proves that the tides are definitely turning in favour of British wine.

For Tom, it's all about the new wave. He explains, 'The first wave of British wine, back around the 1960s, was all about hybrid varieties. The idea around quality was: if it grows, that's good enough. Then came the second wave, which was all about high-quality sparkling, like Nyetimber.' Now, according to Tom, we're very much in the next wave, where styles are taking inspiration from often overlooked old-school winemaking techniques in Europe, seen in the likes of Tillingham's (p.42) Georgian qveri and Juran flor or Matt Gregory's (p.202) field blends.

This new wave is Gnarly Vines' sweet spot. There is always space on their shelves for those maverick producers making, as they say, 'authentic' wines, like Ham Street Wines from Kent and Wiltshire's Offbeat (p.196). Often organic or biodynamic, the British wines at Gnarly Vines are from independently owned vineyards and made gently by small, close-knit teams. The styles themselves range wildly, with some fairly clean and classic examples from leading lights like Davenport (p.68) alongside energetic pét-nats and even alcohol-free wine alternatives.

The wines can all be opened immediately and enjoyed at the communal table with a slice of local favourite Yard Sale pizza or in the secluded garden among the ferns and festoon lighting. For now, there is only one Gnarly Vines but hopefully, before too long, we'll start to see more shops pop up across the UK as new British wine really takes off.

LEFT:
A bottle of Offbeat
Prospect: a blend of
Bacchus, Solaris, Orion,
Madeleine Angevine
and Phoenix, made in
Wiltshire by Daniel and
Nicola Ham (p.196).

One of central London's finest dining rooms, where English sparkling stands proud alongside first-rate Champagne

Berners Tavern

One of the most decadent places to sample a glass of English sparkling is at Berners Tavern, an opulent restaurant occupying the spectacular ballroom of the London EDITION hotel in Fitzrovia, where not so long ago native wines would have had a hard time holding their own against their continental counterparts. Now, however, English sparkling wine is as much at home here as it is on the lists of some of the capital's most prestigious restaurants, from the Chiltern Firehouse to Le Gavroche.

Berners Tavern is huge, yet intimate, unfolding beneath an ornate, Grade-II listed ceiling and surrounded by hundreds of gilt frames which scatter the walls with eclectic art pieces. Enveloped in the gauzy glow of candlelight, the glitterati of London rub shoulders as they pore over the menu and take their pick of the wine list.

The menu is taken care of by Michelin-starred chef Jason Atherton and leans, in joyful juxtaposition to the space's glitz and glamour, towards proper British comfort food. The delight of being able to order a pork pie or fish and chips in London's most ostentatious dining room is matched only by the sheer, gratifying silliness of hailing a champagne trolley for a glass of bubbles – because what else could possibly do? No matter which iconic British dish you choose, the 'Champagne' trolley has just the thing...

Riding pride of place between Champagne monarchs Dom Perignon and Ruinart, sits a bottle of Nyetimber Classic Cuvée, a sparkling wine from the South Downs of England. It's a blend of the three classic Champagne grape varieties – Chardonnay, Pinot Noir and Pinot Meunier, plucked from vineyards across Sussex, Hampshire

'The minerality and freshness you find with English wines tells us about the terroir. England is doing a very good job in terms of quality.'

GIUSEPPE D'ANIELLO, PICTURED LEFT

and Kent – made following the same traditional method as its famous French peers. Graceful, even delicate at first taste – layers of citrus peel, baked apple and almond, fresh pastry and a hint of white blossom reveal a wine that's poised yet powerful in its depth. It's not hard to see why it's collected so many awards over the years. Ever since its Classic Cuvée landed the title Best Sparkling Wine in the World back in 1998, Nyetimber has enjoyed almost three decades of admiration.

'English sparkling is good to have next to Champagne,' Giuseppe D'Aniello, head sommelier of Berners Tavern and one of the judges of the London Wine Competition, tells me. 'The acidity is slightly higher, so it's cleaner, and more precise.'

TOP:
Berners Tavern's most in-demand dish, an indulgent mac and cheese with poached lobster, is paired with Nyetimber's Classic Cuvée from the 'Champagne' trolley, below.

MIDDLE:
Giuseppe D'Aniello, head sommelier, with a bottle of Henners Barrel Chardonnay, one of the English wines on their list.

And sparkling wines aren't the only English bottles to have made the cut. Giuseppe's wine list has a small section dedicated to still wines from the UK, covering both white and red varieties. Bride Valley Chardonnay from Dorset is light and crisp, charged with an almost Chablis-style minerality, while the barrel-aged Henners Chardonnay from Sussex is richer, with stone fruit and toasty, buttery notes. South Devon's Sharpham Pinot Noir, with its mouthwatering hedgerow berries, is a fine example of the kind of light red that seems to work so well in our temperate climate. 'The minerality and freshness you find with these wines tells us about the terroir. England is doing a very good job in terms of quality.'

In just a few short years, English wines have risen from relative obscurity – a quirky listing on a particularly adventurous wine list – to gracing some of London's finest dining rooms. By captivating the attention and highly trained palates of the city's leading sommeliers, they've truly earned their position.

And, as I tuck into a plate of sumptuous mac and cheese crowned with poached lobster, noting how the Nyetimber Classic Cuvée's particular, English acidity cuts through the glorious fattiness of the cheese and fine bubbles cleanse the palate, I can see why this pairing has become one of the restaurant's most iconic, and feel a prickle of excitement for what might be yet to come.

The seaside restaurant making waves with new British wines

Angela's

In the characterful coastal town of Margate, Lee Coad and Charlotte Forsdike set up Angela's, a restaurant serving fresh-from-the-boat seafood that has already earned a far-reaching reputation for its inventive menu and stunning views out across the sea and sandy beach. Stark and utilitarian against the kaleidoscopic backdrop of the main parade, Angela's provides the perfect canvas to highlight locally sourced ingredients and carefully chosen British wine. Recently, Lee and Charlotte also set up a smaller, more casual

seafood bar just around the corner called Dory's, which serves up raw, pickled, cured and baked seafood and has its own bottle shop too, selling biodynamic and low-intervention wines.

Vegetables sourced from local growers, butter and cheese from nearby dairies and, of course, fish caught by intrepid fishermen come together to create a daily changing menu of small plates. The morning's catch is scrawled on the blackboard alongside rock oysters, smoked prawns, lobster toast, mussels cooked in cider and mackerel with pickled cucumber. And it's not just about 'local' produce either, every element of the restaurant has been thoughtfully considered in terms of its sustainability. 'I designed both Angela's and Dory's interiors around the idea of reusing materials,' Lee tells me. 'As with the food, nothing goes to waste.'

The combination of uncomplicated cooking and clean, simple presentation allows the freshness of the ingredients to shine through. The flavours work well with local wine, like the melt-in-the-mouth Whitstable oysters which pair so well with a glass of Davenport Horsmonden (p.68), an aromatic floral white with a mineral edge, grown just a couple of hours' drive from the coast. Or a red field blend of Pinot Noir, Pinot Meunier and Chardonnay from Westwell in Kent (p.118), to savour alongside a plate of lightly fried scallops and crunchy samphire.

'Will Davenport's wines have been on our list since we first opened over five years ago,' Lee says. 'It was the first still wine from England that we felt could belong on any wine list in the country, and definitely belonged on ours. Will is as careful in the vineyard as he is in the winery, it's very apparent that many of Britain's cool young winemakers have sought his wise words over the years. He really is the father of low-intervention still winemaking in England.'

The wine list features an ever-changing selection of bottles, but there's always an impressive array of English wines. Lee and Charlotte fell for their vivacity and remarkable quality while scouring nearby counties for farm produce to cook up at Angela's. Making regular pit stops at vineyards they would find along the way, they realised that English wine was the perfect match for fresh seafood.

'English wine is such an important part of what we do,' explains Lee. 'It feeds into our ethos of keeping it local and reducing waste, but most importantly, it is a great accompaniment to seafood. It gives our restaurants a context, a sense of place, and customers really respond to that.'

'It doesn't get much better than sitting next to the sea eating a freshly caught Margate lobster, drinking a beautifully balanced glass of English Chardonnay,' Lee enthuses. It is extremely hard to disagree.

'English wine is such an important part of what we do. It feeds into our ethos of keeping it local and reducing waste, but most importantly, it is a great accompaniment to seafood.'

LEE COAD

139

The urban winery revelling in breaking conventions

Renegade Urban Winery

Producers in more traditional regions might be bound by strict rules and regulations, controlling everything from what grapes can be planted where, to how long a wine must be aged before it can be released. But British winemakers aren't held back by any historic rules and the team at Renegade Urban Winery are definitely revelling in their freedom. Their rebellious attitude shouts from their disruptive releases, eye-catching labels that pay homage to local Londoners, and alternative

formats, like the tongue-in-cheek 'canpaign-method' sparkling wine sold in recyclable cans.

Renegade started life beneath the railway arch of a graffitied alleyway in Bethnal Green in 2016, but its rapid success meant that they soon outgrew the space. Taking over a new, bigger site on Blackhorse Road, they join a cluster of small-scale breweries and independent bars – a boozy wonderland in E17 – but the original Bethnal Green space is still open as a bar and kitchen and doubles up nicely as a space for wines to age in barrel.

Warwick Smith takes a bottle from a crate of resting wines and tips it, bottoms up, sending tiny particles of grape must and yeasts tumbling towards the crown cap. Still fermenting, the rhubarb-red juice fizzes with energy – energy that will absorb into the wine and become bubbles, before the bottle is released as Renegade Winery's

140

> 'We lean towards a low-intervention winemaking style: wild fermentations, low sulphur, fruit from vineyards that are organic... But we're not making "natural" wines. If we want to correct something, we will.'
>
> WARWICK SMITH

Crystal Nat Fizz. The name stands for pét-nat – the low-intervention sparkling wines sweeping the nation. Almost opaque and deep in colour, Renegade's version is an unconventional wine from an unconventional winery.

Searching for something more soulful after 15 years in financial services, Warwick was ready for a change – and felt that London might be ready for it too. 'I knew nothing about making wine,' he confesses. 'When I hired our first winemaker, he said, "Okay, what sort of wine do you want to make?" and I said, just really good shit.'

'And then he asked, "Yeah, but what style? Do you want filtered, unfiltered, oaked, clean, cold-fermented, inoculated yeast, wild yeast..." I was like, I don't know! So, our philosophy has changed quite a lot since then.'

In their winery, grapes grown by farmers across England and Europe have been plucked from their vineyards, and are now being transformed behind the gleam of spotless stainless steel tanks that stretch out in front of a state-of-the-art press. 'I learnt then that winemaking is a combination of agriculture and science,' Warwick reflects.

Renegade's current winemaker, Andrea Bontempo, spent his formative years in the industry following conventional winemaking. He grew up in the hills of Italy's Prosecco region and completed a degree in viticulture and enology, before working vintages around the world, including at Simpsons Wine Estate in Kent. Embracing the Renegade way of things here in London, he's now getting to grips with lesser-known grapes, like Bacchus, and creating new, experimental styles.

'We lean towards an additive-free winemaking style: wild fermentations, low sulphur, fruit from vineyards that are organic or at least working towards that,' Warwick explains. 'But we're not making "natural" wines. If we want to correct something, we will.' While some winemakers are strictly hands-off when it comes to any chemical intervention (even if it means that the resulting wine might be a little funky), Renegade are more practical and will intervene if they have to.

Lining the shelves around Renegade's tasting room, bottles vary in range and style, from the bright German-grown Alex Riesling to the copper-coloured Araceli Pinot Grigio Ramato rosé (which has a touch of spice and wild cherry, as well as a

LEFT:
Grape juice from the bottom of the stainless steel fermentation tank is pumped back over the skins so that it absorbs more colour and texture.

unique tannic structure from time spent in contact with the grape skins). Another skin-contact wine, the hazy but surprisingly floral Rahul, made from Herefordshire-grown Bacchus grapes, gets its distinctive amber colour from spending a mammoth five months on skins, three of which were in traditional qvevri. There's also a medley of reds sourced from across Europe, all laying in rest in various steel tanks and oak barrels around the winery.

Perhaps Renegade's most out-there creation of all is a release that blurs the boundaries of 'wine' altogether: Bethnal Bubbles is made from grapes, perhaps zesty Seyval Blanc one year, or fruity Pinot Noir another, fermented under hops so that it takes on the dry citrus and even tropical notes of an IPA. Part wine, part craft beer, and completely unique, it's the kind of experimental free-wheeling that can only happen in a wine region unbound by rules.

To this progressive team, British winemaking means taking risks. As Patrick Marriott, one of the winemaking team, points out, 'All the stuff that's now considered traditional, and acceptable, was innovative 50 to 100 hundred years ago.'

Who knows what winemaking in Britain will look like in another 50 years. With these renegades at the press, we know it won't be boring.

VISIT
Renegade Urban Winery
Unit 7
Lockwood Way
London
E17 5RB

SOCIAL
@renegadeurbanwinery

WEBSITE
renegadelondonwine.com

BOTTLES OF NOTE:

BETHNAL BUBBLES 3.1
(PINOT NOIR DRY HOPPED WITH
SABRO, CITRA AND MOSAIC), 2021
Punchy and refreshing like a hoppy IPA with a lovely acidity and aromas of tropical fruits. It's hazy and a bit lively so make sure it's icy cold to avoid it foaming over.

JAMIE NAT FIZZ (BACCHUS), 2021
A dry white wine with notes of elderflower and apricot. Aromatic and fresh, this is a new kind of distinctly English sparkling wine.

The wine bar providing a platform for small-volume producers

Bench

Think of the cities at the forefront of the British wine scene and Sheffield might not be the first place to spring to mind, but over the last five years, one pioneering restaurateur has been leading the charge. Jack Wakelin launched Bench, a neighbourhood wine bar and shop with high-brow cocktails and lo-fi beats, with chef Tom 'Ronnie' Aronica in the summer of 2020 and it's already become the home of a growing community of wine-aficionados in the north of England.

RIGHT:
Co-founders Jack Wakelin and Tom Aronica, each with a glass of Tillingham's (p.42) Field Blend Two.

Before Bench, Jack and Ronnie ran the prestigious cocktail bar Public together, out of a converted gents toilets underneath a Victorian town hall. It was an atmospheric and popular location which went on to be crowned Observer Food Monthly's 'Best Place to Drink in the UK' in 2018, but the constraints of the small underground bar left them wanting to do more.

'There came a point where we wanted to push our boundaries, to create something new and fresh,' Jack explains over oysters and a glass of orange wine as we sit outside on the terrace – which they've playfully coined the Bench Riviera.

'The concept and the name "Bench" are intertwined,' Jack continues, 'we loved the idea of a communal table bringing people together.' Pushing boundaries doesn't have to mean you're doing something avant-garde or challenging – in this

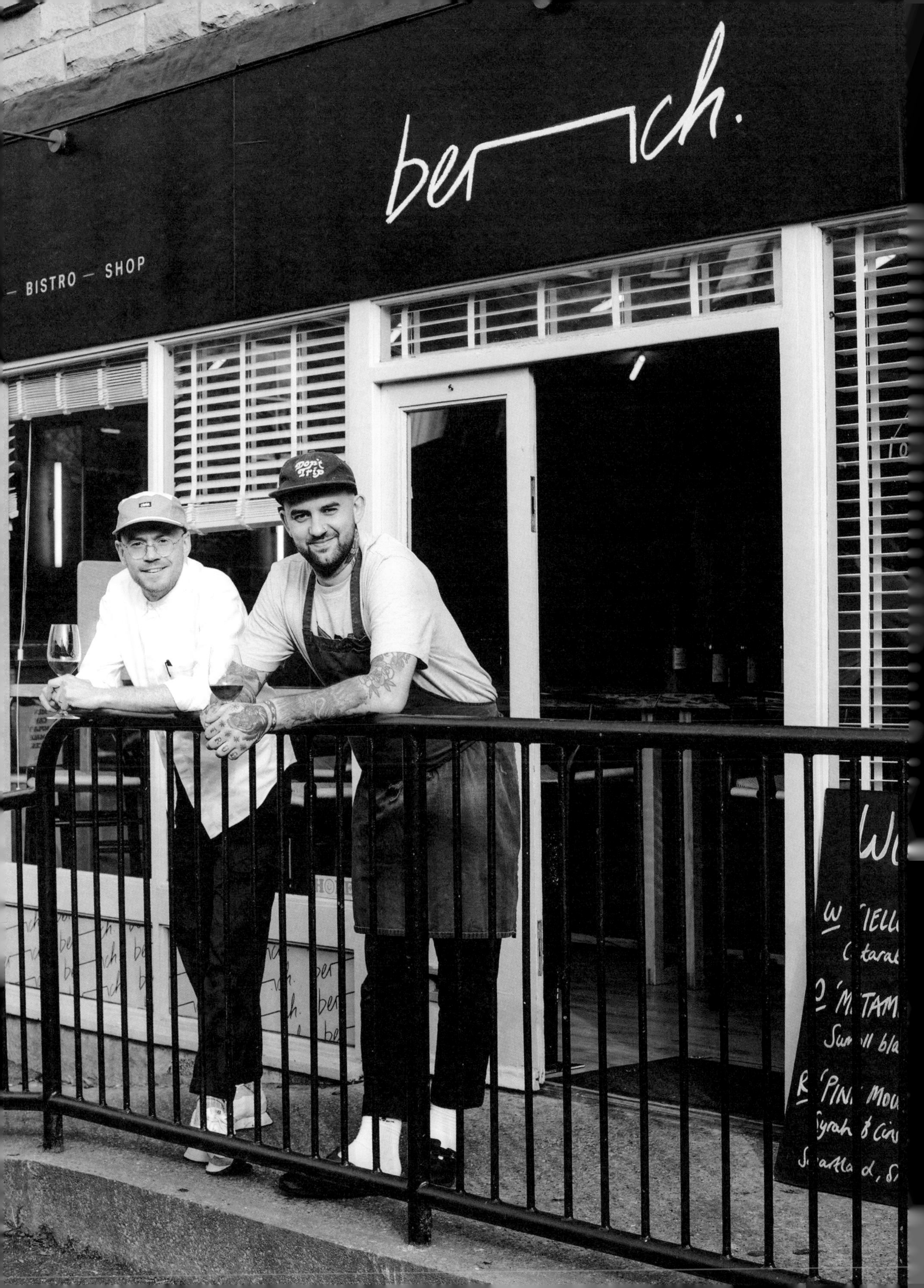
— BISTRO — SHOP

'Opening a bottle, getting people to try new things – changing people's perceptions. It's exciting.'

JACK WAKELIN, PICTURED LEFT

case, it just meant exploring something that isn't the norm yet. Casual, informal places serving artisanal wine around one huge communal table. 'We wanted it to feel like coming round to Ronnie's for tea.'

Bench combines smooth service with an inventive menu and a wine list brimming with new wave wines from small-volume, big-reputation growers across Europe, like skin-contact Sauvignon from the Loire's Sébastien Riffault and old vine Chardonnay from cult Burgundian Frédéric Cossard. The world of wine was a new frontier for Jack when he started Public, and he quickly found himself disillusioned with the larger commercial wineries he visited in Europe. The enthusiasm for wine he has today was sparked by an epiphany, and a vineyard much closer to home, when a visit to Tillingham (p.42) in Sussex showed him that there is another way to make high-quality wine, as well as revealing the serious potential of English producers.

'They'd just finished planting the vines,' Jack remembers. 'They were still laying concrete foundations for the winery and building the cellars. It was a building site!' he laughs. 'But we saw that they were a small team who cared about the land, making wine by hand. And it kind of hit home. We want Bench to be a platform not just for us to talk about cocktails, or food, but also for people growing grapes and making wine.'

For Jack, the wines on the list are as much about the human story behind the bottle as the liquid inside. 'We love wines from Ancre Hill (p.78) in Wales as well – I mean, Albariño grapes grown in Monmouthshire, it's mind-blowing.' Albariño grapes – known for making zesty, saline white wines – are rarely found outside of Portugal or northern Spain so to see the vines flourishing in the Welsh valleys is quite a sight.

'It's always interesting to pour something like Ancre Hill for customers and then compare it with other examples of Albariño from Spain or Portugal. These wines give us something different, and they make a great talking point. With an Albariño from the Iberian peninsula, we might have something like a light wine, with nectarines, lemon zest, bundles of acidity and more often than not plenty of salinity. The Albariño Orange Wine from Ancre Hill not only comes from the most unexpected region, but it's also aged for somewhere between 30 and 50 days on the grape skins. It's completely different: textured, savoury and herbal, but at only 9 percent it's light too.'

'You know, being in Sheffield, where it might not have a massive wine culture yet, it's really important to have fun stuff on the list that people can engage with. Opening a bottle, getting people to try new things – changing people's perceptions. It's exciting.'

Britain's original urban winery tucked away in a Victorian warehouse

London Cru

The former gin distillery and warehouse that houses London Cru's winery might date back to the Victorian era, but when Cliff Roberson installed stainless steel tanks and a grape press in 2012, it became the site of decidedly modern winemaking.

As the founder of Roberson Wine, a fine wine merchant that selects the best bottles from all over the world, Cliff has never been afraid to take risks. He started selling wine in Soho in the early 1960s before spending a few years in Bordeaux and New York (working in Manhattan's fabled Sherry-Lehmann wine store, which included Salvador Dalí

and Andy Warhol among its many customers). On returning to the UK in the 1970s, he brought back wines that were almost unheard of at the time – importing from Chile and California.

Decades later, when he came across an empty warehouse sandwiched between Earl's Court and Fulham Broadway, he knew just what to do with it. He founded London Cru, and in doing so set up the UK's first urban winery. It's within wineries that grapes are pressed, fermented and turned into wine. While many vineyards have their own on-site winery, it's also common practice for 'négociant' winemakers to buy in grapes from vineyards they have good relationships with and bottle them under their own name. It is key to make sure the fruit arrives as fresh and close to being picked as possible.

Bringing winemaking into the city was a bold move, but Cliff had already observed a

RIGHT:
Winemaker Alex Hurley
(on left) and founder
Cliff Roberson outside
the winery.

152

burgeoning movement of urban winemaking unfold in California. Winemakers in San Francisco, San Diego and even LA had started setting up wineries in the unlikeliest of buildings, from decommissioned naval bases to old gas stations, and buying in grapes from vineyards in the surrounding wine country.

'When we built London Cru in 2012, there was nothing else like it in the UK,' explains Cliff. 'We looked at this empty warehouse and it had the same sort of energy as those places we'd seen in California. So we thought, "Well, we should make wine here."'

'Ten years ago, a lot of English wines were terrible,' he reflects. 'And it was expensive to make, which meant it was expensive to drink.' But he'd seen that urban wineries didn't need to be close to vineyards in order to make good wine. So, when London Cru began production, they started by sourcing grapes from growers across Europe (mostly in Italy, France and Spain) – and the results were impressive, showing that urban wineries have real potential, not just in sunny California but also in south London.

Now, London Cru sources grapes exclusively from English vineyards. It allows them to support local growers, reduces the environmental impact of transport and means the grapes can be plucked from the vineyard and pressed in the winery within a matter of hours. This change of direction is a testament to the ever-rising standard of British vineyards; 'In my opinion the quality will keep getting better,' says Cliff, 'I really think we're onto something.'

London Cru's 2019 Traditional Method Sparkling (made from 100 percent Pinot Meunier grown in Canterbury), with its rich spectrum of notes from stone fruit to toasty biscuits, is opulent and refined; two years of ageing on lees (spent yeast) in oak barrels lend the extra depth and texture that you'd expect from top-tier sparklings. As the first sparkling to be released by winemaker Alex Hurley since joining London Cru from esteemed UK producer Gusbourne, it's a serious example of what England can do.

Hailing from Australia, Alex has worked in a number of highly regarded, international wineries with cult followings, including Barolo's G.D. Vajra and Le Grappin in Burgundy. Along the way he also completed a master's in viticulture and enology in France. It was there that he had his first taste of English sparkling wine, although he didn't know it at the time, as friends on the course would sneak samples of Nyetimber and Gusbourne into the tastings, disguised as Champagne.

'I really liked them, and eventually found my way to England. Working at Gusbourne, I learnt their way of doing things. When it comes to traditional-method sparklings, people have high expectations. There's a certain flavour profile they need to hit.'

Classic traditional-method sparkling wines should show bright, clear liquid, pale lemon to gold in colour, with fine but persistent bubbles. The flavours should be balanced – fresh and clean, but with interest and complexity; showing fruit alongside richer notes. It should be elegant and never overpowering, with a long, lingering sensation.

Alex's experience shines through in the sparkling wines he makes at London Cru, and bottles are snapped up by some of the top restaurants in the country, including Michelin-starred spots in London. 'We sell to a lot of sommeliers so the wines have to be clean, textured and gastronomic. It's great to be able to show the world that we can make that style, but it's nice to produce other, more experimental sparklings too.'

'They are pushing the boundaries, doing things differently and exploring... I think that in a few years England is going to be making the most innovative and interesting wine in the world.'

ALEX HURLEY, PICTURED RIGHT

Alongside these traditional-method sparklings, within the London Cru range you'll also find still wines and some lively pét-nats. These sparkling wines are made outside the strict boundaries of the traditional method used to craft Champagne, allowing winemakers to develop something new. London Cru's Pinot Gris Pét-nat 2021, inspired by Portugal's spritzy Vinho Verde and the Txakoli wines of northern Spain, tingles with lime zest and wild savoury flavours, with an intriguing flint note that's there for a second and then gone

'Pét-nat can be anything,' Alex says. 'Its creativity and discipline are two sides of the same coin.' Alex's studies in enology have given him a deep understanding of the winemaking process, and he lights up when talking about the various intricacies of flavour creation, from working with different yeast parcels to encourage specific aromas and flavours to using oak to soften a wine in a cool vintage, or stainless steel to highlight freshness during warmer years. It's this enthusiasm for the complexity and precision of winemaking that drew him to the new wine scene developing in Britain.

'In the UK, people are planting all these different varieties,' says Alex. 'They are pushing the boundaries, doing things differently and exploring. That's what makes it so exciting. I think that in a few years England is going to be making the most innovative and interesting wine in the world.'

VISIT
London Cru Winery
Seagrave Road
London
SW6 1RP

SOCIAL
@londoncru

WEBSITE
londoncru.co.uk

BOTTLES OF NOTE:

BACCHUS 2021
Crisp and aromatic dry white with gooseberry and a crisp bite, as well as hints of grassy notes. Creamy but well balanced by fresh acidity. As the vintage was cooler, malolactic fermentation was partially completed to add complexity and a softer finish.

PINOT NOIR PRÉCOCE 2021
This Pinot has raspberry, strawberry and rhubarb. The wine has soft tannins and captures the lively, fruity style of the Précoce grape while still being serious, taut and tense.

The one-acre vineyard where grapes thrive in a walled garden

Charlie Herring

Part of the allure of wine is its ability to express a sense of place, or terroir – every bottle can tell a story of where and when it was made. Pay close attention and it will give clues of a specific soil and slope, of farmland, coast or mountain, as well as the weather the grapes have endured through the year. The wines created by Tim Phillips, a former accountant turned avant-garde winemaker, speak of their own peculiarly unique microclimate.

Tim set up his vineyard and winery, called Charlie Herring, in an abandoned 19th-century

RIGHT:
Tim Phillips, the sole owner, grape-grower and winemaker of Charlie Herring, with his trusty vineyard assistants.

walled garden in Lymington, just two miles from where the Solent meets the sea. The name was inspired by his father: 'Somewhere in between being a wine merchant and a vicar, my father used to draw old cartoons, and he would sign them off by scribbling the name Charlie Herring. For me, it's about the values I hold, instilled by my parents, that guide everything I do in life. I like to think that anyone else connected by the same values is as much Charlie Herring as I am.'

The vineyard is near enough to the sea that a warm maritime breeze is inhaled by the stone walls (which also protect the vines from storms or frost), making the air within noticeably, pleasantly mild. Mild enough that even the fussiest of grape varieties can feel at home. Rows of Sauvignon Blanc vines dig happily into the gravel soils, their grapes basking alongside the more familiar

Chardonnay, while a tangle of Riesling vines climb freely across the wall. This sense of warmth and richness radiates from the aromas of Charlie Herring's wines, the grapes showing a healthy ripeness and concentration of flavours even though Tim grows them much further north than they would usually be planted.

Tim is the sole grower and maker behind Charlie Herring, having stumbled across the derelict Victorian walled garden by chance while cycling to his parents' house. 'When I first walked through the door, it was so overgrown that it took two full days just to reach the other side,' he recalls. The garden had been neglected for so long that it had grown into a wild abandon of flora and fauna, so Tim busily set about regenerating the land – coppicing the orchard, bedding in tea plants and flowers and establishing a compost heap. In 2008, he planted his first vines. 'I didn't know what would grow, so I planted the varieties I liked,' He tells me. 'I like Chardonnay, I adore Riesling. Down by the port you can get fresh day-caught crab, and I thought how nice it would be to drink my own Sauvignon Blanc... I had absolutely no idea whether they'd work or not.'

Don't be fooled by the laissez-faire attitude. It belies a deep and intricate knowledge of winemaking. Tim made the switch from spreadsheets to wine two decades ago, leaving England for the vineyards of South Africa, where he studied viticulture and enology, and ended up spending the best part of ten years making wine around the world before eventually returning home to Hampshire. He reflects, 'The connection to the land is what pulled me back. There's something that physically roots me in the English soil, and the New Forest, which is where I was brought up.'

This innate connection to his homeland led Tim to plant vines in England, where the wines show a freshness not found in the other regions he'd worked in. However, his dedication to growing organically presented a challenge: 'Being organic in England is hard,' he admits. 'We see it in the cooler vintages especially – natural crops will show the signs, while non-organic will look the same as any other year. But those growers are spraying chemicals and that's not something I can ever do.'

When we visit, one early autumn morning, four hens are busy scratching and foraging for food amid the greenery surrounding a Victorian glasshouse. Behind, an archway leads out of the kitchen garden through to an ancient orchard of apple and pear trees, and the last remains of a 1920s tennis court besieged by weeds and moss.

Tim's holistic approach is also applied to his winemaking. Not far from the walled garden lies a thriving woodland brimming with wildlife. Somewhere among the trees is a garage, and it's here that Tim crafts tiny batches of limited-releases: various blends of Chardonnay; Riesling aged until softened and mellow; perhaps a subtly-spiced Sauvignon Blanc – the style all depends on where the wines themselves lead in that particular year.

'Down by the port you can get fresh day-caught crab, and I thought how nice it would be to drink my own Sauvignon Blanc... I had absolutely no idea whether they'd work or not.'

TIM PHILLIPS

'For me, it's about the values I hold, instilled by my parents, that guide everything I do in life. I like to think that anyone else connected by the same values is as much Charlie Herring as I am.'

TIM PHILLIPS, PICTURED RIGHT

In 2020, Tim made his first still wine from Riesling and called it Promised Land. It is one of the only single varietal still Rieslings in the UK and brims with citrus, white pepper and an enlivening touch of salinity. Charlie Herring wines can be difficult to track down, each vintage getting snapped up quickly as Tim makes them in such small quantities, just 2000 bottles each year (to put this into context, even an independent, organic vineyard will usually produce around 30,000 bottles). However, the ciders that he presses from red apples harvested from the ancient apple trees in his orchard are a little easier to get your hands on. His Perfect Strangers Vin ed Pom is inspired by an almost obsolete northern Italian tradition of fermenting apples alongside grape pomace (the skins and pulp left over after the fruits have been pressed for wine), giving the cider a distinctive red tint and a hint of berry that complements the earthiness of the apple.

If temperatures in the UK continue to rise, we might start to see more vineyards like Charlie Herring planting grapes typically suited to warmer climates, such as Sauvignon Blanc and Riesling. But there are other factors to consider too – soil types, PH levels, moisture levels, altitude – all of which determine what we can and can't grow in Britain. And that's without considering how rising temperatures might wreck our ecosystems and cause more extreme weather events, neither of which would be good for vineyards. We are still at the beginning of British winemaking, but, hopefully, regardless of what the future brings, there will be more vignerons like Tim Phillips to lead the way.

VISIT
Charlie Herring
Yaldhurst Lane
Lymington
Hampshire
SO41 8HE

SOCIAL
@charlieherringwines

WEBSITE
charlieherring.com

BOTTLE OF NOTE:

PERFECT STRANGERS (95 PERCENT APPLES, 5 PERCENT WINE)
Apples from Tim's ancient apple trees are fermented on grape skins, adding a splash of colour and a distinctive note of red berries. This wine-cider hybrid is based on a northern Italian specialty: *vid ed pom*.

TOP:
Tim discovered an old
Victorian greenhouse
in the walled garden,
which he now uses to
propagate new vines
from existing stock.

The destination restaurant cultivating a list of thoughtfully produced British wine

People travel from across the country for a table at Osip, the 22-seat Michelin-starred, farm-led restaurant that occupies an old ironmonger's in the historic market town of Bruton, Somerset. Within the utilitarian dining room, all antique floorboards and clean white walls, the menu reflects the same refined simplicity and celebrates local produce with a quiet reverence. Alongside the menu is a thoughtfully composed wine list, a compact curation of growers (many of them local) who pour the same level of respect into the land that Osip does.

RIGHT:
The menu at Osip is centred on vegetables and wild herbs grown on plots of land belonging to owner and chef Merlin Labron-Johnson.

'We get inspired by winemakers all around the world that we feel aligned with,' explains Merlin Labron-Johnson (pictured overleaf), the owner and chef. Merlin was raised in Devon before he left to work in Michelin-starred kitchens across Europe, pausing in London to open two acclaimed restaurants in quick succession, Portland and Clipstone, which are both thriving today. He then followed his roots back to the rural south-west of England to open Osip, and, just next door, The Old Pharmacy; a wine bar, café and deli serving rustic small plates influenced by the unfussy flavours of northern Italy and rural Provence. 'Grandma cuisine' as it's affectionately called by the team.

'We have a preoccupation with growing our own vegetables, with seasonality and locality,' Merlin says. Both Osip and The Old Pharmacy are supplied by two plots of land where they grow

'What's lovely about English wine is that it's already a synthesis of our local surroundings... the act of pairing a food with a wine is already, in part, performed for us.'

MERLIN LABRON-JOHNSON, PICTURED LEFT

their own vegetables. The daily changing menu is a showcase of the season's finest work: young leeks in spring; courgette flowers with lovage; gnudi made from ricotta from the local dairy, or wild mushrooms topped with thinly sliced lardo in the darker months.

'There is a strong link between our mentality towards food and our treatment of the wine lists at Osip and The Old Pharmacy,' explains Merlin. This link comes through in the small but perfectly formed selection of organic and low-intervention bottles, like Domaine Hugo (p.196), a sparkling wine produced from biodynamically grown grapes in nearby Wiltshire. Sommelier Bobby Taylor pours a glass, aromas of fresh blossom and citrus being released with each pop of a bubble. 'It's brilliantly savoury,' says Bobby. Although working with nearby wine producers fits with the restaurant's wider ethos, there's no special treatment here – it all comes back to quality. Merlin adds, 'The wines only make it onto the list if they can match up to the quality of the bottles either side of them on the rack... We like to work with British producers because they are local to us, but they have to really prove the point that British wine has the potential to be special while also being produced considerately.'

Domaine Hugo (p.196) is a biodynamic wine, produced using pre-industrial farming techniques carried out in accordance with the rhythms of nature, that aim to restore the health of soil that would otherwise be damaged by intensive agriculture. 'What's lovely about English wine,' Merlin reflects, 'is that it's already a synthesis of

our local surroundings... There's a philosophy many people subscribe to that often informs my cooking – what grows together will taste good together. With English wine, the act of pairing a food with a wine is already, in part, performed for us.' A glass of sparkling from Domaine Hugo is one the team recommends at the start of a meal, and goes gloriously well with a plate of warm, light-as-air cheese gougères, 'preferably made using Westcombe cheddar,' Merlin adds. 'Baked gougères have a toasted flavour which complements the buttery, brioche-like bubbles, while the saltiness from the cheese accentuates the fruit and aromas in the wine.' It's the kind of simple but effective pairing that comes together perfectly, forming one of life's little pleasures.

Another English wine on their list is Westwell's Pelegrim NV, (p.118) which Bobby praises for its 'balance of energetic orchard fruit and lasting acidity.' Made from grapes grown on the chalk and fossil-rich soils of Kent's Pilgrim Way, it's a crisp and cool sparkling with fragrant notes of baked apple and acacia honey.

Britain may be home to one of the fastest-growing wine regions in the world, but we're still in the early days and it's very much an emerging industry. While there are those in the know, there are also still hordes of restaurants across the UK as yet unaware of what's available on their own doorstep. Osip may be a tiny restaurant, but it has a big reputation. By showcasing British bottles, they are communicating their beauty and quality to others all across the country.

169

The independent vigneron ripping up the rule book

Dunleavy Vineyards

It takes guts, resilience and dogged determination to run a vineyard in the UK. Luckily Ingrid Bates, the woman behind Dunleavy Vineyards, has as much grit as the UK has rain. Dunleavy sits snug among the lush farmlands of Somerset's Yeo Valley, flanked by the wax-jacket green of the West Country farmlands where Ingrid was born and raised. Unlike most winemakers, she came to the world of wine not through her admiration of the liquid, but through a love of nature – having studied biology and worked as a researcher in the BBC's Natural History Unit before turning her green fingers to vines.

RIGHT:
Ingrid Bates, viticulturalist and owner of Dunleavy Vineyards, pictured with her dog, Fly.

Ingrid had the dream and desire to grow grapes; all that was missing were some vineyards. In 2008, while she was still in her 20s, Ingrid took a leap into the unknown and leased just a little over two acres of land. Most growers will only plant vines on land they own, firstly because vines take years to come of age to produce anything wine-worthy, and secondly, it's such a temperamental crop. Ingrid, however, refused to be put off and started small with just one wine – a rosé made from a blend of Pinot Noir and Seyval Blanc, which flows with notes of strawberry and peach.

'For the first few years, we just made rosé because that was all I could afford to make!' Ingrid reminisces as we weave between rows of vines, white and red grapes plump on their stems. Ingrid's dog, Fly, scampers ahead, occasionally stopping to nose the soil. It's solitary work, tending the vines

'Grapes like these thrive in our climate, they're really happy here. And they allow us to gradually shift to a gentler, less interventionist vineyard.'

INGRID BATES

alone, but Fly makes an entertaining assistant, if not a particularly competent one. The vineyard area is small in comparison to others producing wines commercially, but it is 'big enough to be scary when it's growing out of control,' Ingrid adds. 'Over the years we've steadily added sparkling whites, then sparkling reds, all in small batches.'

The stand-out wines that come out of Dunleavy now are the result of Ingrid's ability to learn as she goes (and grows), experimenting along the way. 'We've been playing with different grapes to see what works. Our first sparkling red, we made with Rondo. People have a strong reaction to its slight earthiness. They either don't quite know what to do with it, or they love it.' The sparkling red is joyful in its difference, and really fun. Light in body with mouthwatering cherry and herb flavours, it makes you think again about what red wine can be.

Another similar experiment is the playfully named Bottom, a sparkling wine made from Seyval Blanc. It is essentially made from the early stages of their traditional-method Brut Sparkling White,

but the lees in the bottom are not disgorged, resulting in a cloudier, tartly savoury wine. Many pét-nats are made in this way, following almost the same method as traditional-method sparkling but left undisgorged. Disgorging is a complex (and expensive) process that involves slowly turning the bottles over and over again until the lees collect in the bottle's neck. Here they are frozen so that they will be expelled when the crown cap is removed. The bottle is then closed with a cork and cage, like Champagne and Prosecco. If a bottle of sparkling wine is topped with a crown cap, it might be a sign that it will be gently fizzy, rather than bursting with bubbles, and might also have finished fermenting in bottle. As Ingrid explains, Bottom could be classed as 'sort of pét-nat, sort of col fondo, depending on who you talk to.' In fact, col fondo, an Italian variant on pét-nat, literally translates to 'with the bottom'.

A few years ago, Ingrid ripped up her old Pinot Noir vines (a famously fickle grape that does do well in England but requires a near relentless amount of time and energy) and replaced them with Rondo. 'It's one of the so-called "untrendy" ones,' she says, adding air quotes. Rondo, one of the modern varietals planted widely in the UK during the first wave of British winemaking, is enjoying a resurgence among younger, less traditional growers. 'Grapes like these thrive in our climate,

175

'It's quite nice that we don't have many rules because we can just sort of faff about and experiment. That's quite fun, isn't it?'

INGRID BATES, PICTURED RIGHT

they're really happy here,' Ingrid enthuses. 'And they allow us to gradually shift to a gentler, less interventionist vineyard.'

Rules and definitions are not something that Ingrid has much time for. Without this originality, she might never have been brave enough to dive into winemaking in the first place. So it's a subject she feels passionate about when it comes to British winemaking, saying, 'I think there are a lot of people who want to make the rules tighter in this country.'

We're at a key point in time, when traditionalists want to standardise permitted grapes and winemaking techniques, pulling the UK more in line with historic winemaking regions like Champagne. The purpose of such regulations would be to protect and conserve quality – but it has the potential to stifle the creativity that we're seeing today. 'Actually, in some ways, it's quite nice that we don't have many rules. We can faff about and experiment, and that's quite fun, isn't it?'

VISIT
Dunleavy Vineyards
Wrington
Bristol
Somerset
BS40 5RS

SOCIAL
@dunleavyvineyards

WEBSITE
dunleavyvineyards.co.uk

BOTTLES OF NOTE:

SPARKLING RED
(RONDO AND PINOT NOIR), 2021
These sparkling reds challenge conventions, which is something Ingrid very much enjoys doing. This wine has all the raspberries, cherries and plums you might expect from Pinot Noir and Rondo, but less rhubarb.

ROSÉ (REGENT AND
SEYVAL BLANC), 2019
This rosé is very versatile and pairs well with anything from Sunday roasts to spicy Indian food, which is why it is on the lists of so many independent restaurants in Bristol.

The family-run vineyard rivalling the best of Champagne

Camel Valley

One of the sparkling wines you can usually expect to find sitting on a shelf at Waitrose, alongside world-famous names like Veuve Clicquot and English powerhouse Nyetimber, hails from a small, family-run vineyard near the Cornish town of Bodmin. Run by one of the only second-generation vignerons in the country, Sam Lindo, it is proof that British wine doesn't have to sell out in order to, well, sell out. Bob and Annie Lindo, Sam's parents, planted Camel Valley's first vines back in 1989.

After two decades flying around the world as an RAF pilot, Bob decided to return to solid ground, and chose the sun-soaked slopes of the idyllic Cornish countryside as the place to put down some roots. Those same slopes just happened to be the perfect place to raise vines, and so Bob and Annie turned their hands to winemaking. Among the first to attempt to make wine commercially in this country, they had little idea that they would become pioneers of a movement that is still booming over 30 years later.

Back in the 1980s, however, it wasn't Champagne-style sparkling wine that excited British winemakers, but styles more akin to the sweeter, cool-climate German white wines fashionable at the time. The first varieties Bob planted were German and Alpine hybrids like Reichensteiner, Triomphe, Seyval Blanc and Léon

Millot, which were robust enough to withstand the Cornish weather. Their inaugural wine was a success, a still white described by critics as 'England's answer to Sancerre' (a French region renowned for its deliciously flinty Sauvignon Blanc), but this early triumph belies just how challenging it was to make quality wine in 20th-century Britain – and often still is. Reminiscing about those early days, Bob says, 'The community was very friendly, but the work was very hard.'

They were humble beginnings. Bob and Annie worked the vineyard by hand and made wine in their garage, but over the years they accrued a purpose-built winery and a dedicated small team. As the team and business grew, so did the range, and their reputation. Partly inspired by the small number of traditional-method sparkling wines that had started to pop up in England – coupled with the realisation that acidities were high for still wines, but perfect for fizz – Bob and Annie started making sparkling wine and the awards came pouring in, cementing their position in the upper echelons of the British wine movement. In 2005, Camel Valley won the International Wine Challenge Gold Medal for their 'Cornwall' sparkling wine, beating world-class Champagnes from France, Franciacortas from Italy and Cavas from Spain. A vivacious sparkling with pert bubbles and hints of wild berry on honey-drizzled toast.

The couple's son, Sam, grew up alongside the vines and, when he was old enough, eventually joined the business. Although in traditional winemaking regions like the Rhône or Piedmont, it's common to hear about second (or even third and fourth) generation winemakers who spent their childhoods happily plucking grapes during harvest and scrambling over barrels, it's still vanishingly rare in Britain's nascent industry.

Sam says, 'While I was growing up, I didn't think it would end up being my career. The business wasn't big enough. My perspective changed when I went to New Zealand and saw how large a winery could be, and how quickly the industry had grown there, and thought maybe Camel Valley could also take over the world. But then we visited the Old World vineyards of France, and when someone tells you about their 100-year-old vineyard you realise there is much more to it than just getting big. It is much more rewarding to create something sustainable over time.'

These days, Sam leads the way with help from his father. 'Without Sam,' Bob tells me, 'my success would have been very short lived.' Together they've made a range of classic, high-quality wines that have earned them an avalanche of awards, and even a much-coveted royal warrant, having supplied the Royal Household with sparkling wine for many years, and yet the family-owned and run winery still retains great charm and soul.

VISIT
Camel Valley
Nanstallon
Bodmin
Cornwall
PL30 5LG

SOCIAL
@camelvalleyvineyard

WEBSITE
camelvalley.com

BOTTLE OF NOTE:

PINOT NOIR ROSÉ BRUT, 2019
A beautifully balanced, light pink traditional-method sparkling wine with a lovely floral and delicate strawberry fruit nose and crisp acidity.

ABOVE:
Bottles of Camel Valley
Pinot Noir Rosé Brut are
labelled. Everything is done
in-house at this family-
run business, co-founded
by Annie Lindo (pictured
right) in the 1980s.

A vineyard with an organic solution to stormy weather

Trevibban Mill

Trevibban Mill is a family-run vineyard only ten minutes drive from the coastal town of Padstow. Although planting vines in Cornwall might be a relatively new phenomenon, the vineyard itself is rooted in land containing layers of local history, from a disused slate quarry to an ancient woodland and a ruined watermill – the old 'Trevibban Mill' itself.

Before leaving London for a new life tending vines and pressing grapes, Liz and Engin Mumcuoglu

RIGHT:
Engin and Liz Mumcuoglu, co-owners of Trevibban Mill, in front of the nets that protect their grapes and allow them to ripen perfectly at lower temperatures.

had high-flying careers in science and business respectively. In 2008, they planted their first vines, and in the years to follow added wildflowers, apple trees, sweet chestnuts and other trees. Soon came their purpose-built winery, and in 2014 Liz and Engin launched their first wine. In the years since they've turned their hands to a range of styles: fizzy pét-nat, complex Chardonnay and brooding reds flow from the winery that sits among the wildflowers.

Biodiversity is at the heart of everything that happens at Trevibban Mill, where Southdown sheep (who can also be found on the labels of their bottles) are left to graze the vineyards and orchards at certain times of year to keep the weeds at bay instead of using herbicides, while solar panels on the roof of the winery generate clean energy. By covering their vines with fine netting and protecting

184

them from the worst of the cold, wind and rain, Liz and Engin have been able to make some exceptionally good English red wines.

One stand-out example is the Black Ram Red, a blend of Dornfelder (a lesser-known modern grape that can make lip-smackingly good dark reds) and Rondo that's full of late summer hedgerows and stonefruit like blackberry, plum and cherry pie. These fruit notes ripen happily thanks to the sheltered position of the vineyard and its south-easterly aspect (as well as the netting), while a hint of minerality peeks through from the slate soil.

Trevibban Mill also has a dry and refreshing cider pét-nat that makes the most of Cornwall's famously good apples. The cider is bottled while it's still fermenting, trapping the energy of the process as delicate bubbles, along with some fine residual lees that add delicious biscuity notes to the gentle, long-lasting fizz. For some, cider is the real Champagne of England – after all, the techniques used to create Champagne-style sparkling are said to have been invented by cidermakers in the West Country in the 17th century. By mixing up the methods used to produce wine and cider, Trevibban Mill is breaking down the superfluous distinctions that sometimes get in the way of a good drink.

'Cornwall is not the easiest place in the UK to grow grapes,' explains Liz. 'The climate's damp, which means the yields are probably lower than they might be in the south-east of England.' But yields are not the focus at Trevibban Mill, instead they are more interested in the quality of the grape and making the best, most characterful wine possible, even if it might be in small quantities.

'What we do have here is a real identity,' Liz continues. 'People come here and they want to eat local seafood, and drink an English wine from Cornwall. I'm not sure you get that everywhere else in the country. Cornwall feels a bit different to the rest of England. It's its own place.'

VISIT
Trevibban Mill Vineyard
Dark Lane
Padstow
Cornwall
PL27 7SE

SOCIAL
@trevibbanmill_vineyard

WEBSITE
trevibbanmill.com

BOTTLES OF NOTE:

BLACK RAM RED
(DORNFELDER AND RONDO), 2019
This wine showcases the nuance of English-grown reds – smooth and balanced, a deep ruby red with a vibrant finish. Aromas of dark chocolate, baked plums with touches of clove, black pepper and black cherry.

CONSTANTINE (CHARDONNAY, 2020)
A notable and unique oaked Chardonnay. It showcases elegance and richness, moderated by a refreshing acidity.

PINOT NOIR ROSÉ SPARKLING, 2019
Standing proudly next to some fabulous examples of sparkling wines around the world, this classic sparkling has depth, richness and a crunchy acidity which all complement the fresh-cut strawberry and cream flavours.

A flock of Southdown
sheep keep weeds at
bay in the orchards and
vineyard. Liz and Engin
illustrate many of their
labels and corks with
their beloved sheep.

The ambitious restaurant and bar with the world's largest selection of British wine

Oxeye

As a chef and restaurateur, Sven-Hanson Britt doesn't just champion British ingredients. Both Oxeye (his fine dining restaurant) and Bar Rex (the adjacent wine bar) in south London's Nine Elms are completely centred on them. On the ever-evolving menu, thoughtfully sourced local produce like wild garlic and hand-dived scallops from Orkney sit alongside global influences like yuzu and truffle; Sven-Hanson knows where everything comes from. Even the tableware and ceramics are made by local craftspeople.

But it's the wine list, a 300-strong selection sourced almost exclusively from across the UK, that really shows their dedication to British producers. The walls of Bar Rex are lined with bottles of varying colours and styles, from traditional sparklings by established vineyards Nyetimber, Gusbourne and Breaky Bottom to more contemporary labels like Forty Hall (p.108) and Renegade (p.140).

It's a bold move to build an entire wine list from a region that's still undiscovered by many. While restaurants focusing on locally sourced food are increasingly common, applying that same approach to the wine selection is still radical. For Sven-Hanson's all-important debut restaurant, it put him years ahead of his peers.

The idea first came to the chef over a decade ago while he was working across vineyards in

> 'We pour stuff made by farmers... Winemakers and growers can give themselves fancy viticultural names and titles, but they're farmers farming something. And we want to find people who happen to do it in a lovely way.'
>
> SVEN-HANSON BRITT

France, and he felt inspired to do the same in England. 'Being from Hampshire, which was becoming a real hotspot for quality English winemaking, it seemed worth checking out.' He ended up joining a small winery, where he worked in the on-site restaurant at night and the vineyard by day. Although the winery eventually closed, for Sven, an idea had been planted. 'The wine from that particular vineyard was... questionable,' he grins, 'but there were others making some fantastic wine. I got to know some lovely people who are now running top vineyards and making great wines, so we have that connection.' And so the desire to shine a spotlight on British wines has been around for as long as Sven's dream of opening a restaurant. But, before doing either, Sven left kitchens altogether.

Just as Sven-Hanson's enthusiasm for wine comes from time spent among the vines, his passion for locally sourced ingredients is rooted in the years he spent renovating and rewilding a farm in Derbyshire. With renewed vigour, Sven, now as co-owner of that farm, made his return to London and opened Oxeye in 2021, sourcing produce from growers he'd met along the way.

LEFT:
One of Oxeye's signature dishes is wild Cornish turbot braised in oxidised English wine and finished with a classic 'Champagne' sauce made with Nyetimber's single vineyard sparkling wine, Tillington.

The arrival of Ben Picart, Oxeye's general manager and sommelier, put Sven-Hanson's ideal British wine list to the test. As a native Frenchman, who spent years pouring high-end wines in Hong Kong's finest restaurants, Ben has discerning taste.

'It was quite nerve-wracking,' Sven admits, concerned as to how Ben's highly trained, and French, palate would appreciate British wine. 'Before the restaurant opened, we went to as many vineyards as possible, buying from the cellar door and filling up the boot of the car. Some of the vineyards are beautiful, others can be a bit rough and ready.'

Ben admits to feeling a little trepidation at first too, but the vineyards soon won him over: 'Before meeting Sven, I had very little idea about English wine. Those wine trips opened up a whole new world, I found it fascinating. Opening a bottle and tasting something new – that's the best part of it.'

'We love seeing guests' reactions and how much people love the wines,' says Ben. 'We try to gauge whether they might be adventurous – will they want something a little bit quirky, or more classic?'

Oxeye and Bar Rex are the perfect places to visit in order to get to grips with the breadth of British wines, whether they're traditional-method sparkling, still whites, barrel-aged reds or cosmopolitan skin-contact orange wines.

'Looking at the English wine scene,' Sven-Hanson reflects, 'the people who make the wine and the people who serve the wine – they are all really passionate about something that's relatively new. They're willing to get out there, do their thing and share it with the world.'

195

The marine biologist who combines scientific know-how with gut instinct

Offbeat Wines

From a tiny winery on Botley Farm in Wiltshire, marine biologists turned winemakers Daniel and Nicola Ham craft micro-batches of English wine to an unorthodox method: low intervention, zero sulphur and from strictly organic grapes. It's an avant-garde outlook that has sommeliers up and down the country paying attention. It's also divisive. For some, Dan is making the most thrilling wines in the UK right now. For others, he's straying too far from the familiar. But either way,

RIGHT:
Offbeat co-founders Daniel and Nicola Ham together with Jarvis the cocker spaniel, in front of their 1970s vintage two-tonne wooden Coquard basket press.

it's undeniable that Offbeat is breaking barriers and successfully producing sell-out wines in a way people thought could never be done in Britain's cool and unreliable climate.

Dan's ruling philosophy is one of simply 'following the wine'. He eschews the insurance of disease prevention sprays in the vineyard and stabilisation techniques in the winery, preferring instead to allow the grapes to ferment and to watch and see how the juice turns out, rather than engineering or manipulating the flavour in any way. It's a courageous method. While the 'hands-off' approach may seem like the easiest option on the surface, it requires a deep understanding of the winemaking process and a gut-load of intuition.

Although Dan sources grapes for Offbeat from a select number of British growers that he knows and trusts to farm well, he also collaborates with

Hugo Stewart, the renowned viticulturist who owns Botley Farm – one of the UK's few biodynamic vineyards – on a very special wine. Using grapes from Botley Farm, Dan and Hugo create Domaine Hugo, a revered traditional-method sparkling that runs as a separate project from Offbeat. With a livening flash of citrus, it's a fine example of how organic and biodynamic wines can defy expectations. Hugo refuses to use synthetic pesticides or fertilisers and, as a biodynamic farmer, he cultivates and harvests in harmony with the lunar calendar, according to techniques developed in the 1920s. A long-time farmer and respected grower, he spent 15 years running a biodynamic estate in the south of France before returning to the UK and applying his expertise to his own vineyard. 'Amazing, even to me, is that the fruit that comes off this vineyard is genuinely the ripest and cleanest I've come across,' enthuses Dan.

Before turning their attention to winemaking, Dan and Nicola were both focused on careers in science. 'Marine biology sounds more glamorous than it is,' Dan says. 'People picture diving with sharks, but I was basically spending eight hours a day examining samples of the seabed under a microscope. At the same time, we were living in New Zealand and visiting all these vineyards and meeting winemakers who looked super happy all the time.'

Dan felt the need for change and, in a now-or-never moment, decided to make the move into wine. He spent three years training at Plumpton College, before working for the well-known sparkling wine powerhouse Ridgeview in Sussex in 2012 and then Langham in Dorset.

'At Ridgeview, I was making 300,000 bottles of sparkling wine, which was really jumping in at the deep end. When a winery gets to that size, it has to be very recipe-led so there's not much creative freedom. At Langham, I started playing with spontaneous fermentation and stopped filtering, as well as only using very low sulphur. Making wine in this way is a risk – you only get one chance a year, otherwise you need to wait for the next vintage.'

At Offbeat, in his own 'garage' winery, Dan can now let his creativity truly run wild. He enthusiastically talks through his winemaking techniques, how they use a method of slow pressing modelled on traditional winemaking in Jura (a region in France recognised as a cult region for natural winemaking). Depending on what the vintage brings, Dan makes wine in a kaleidoscopic range of styles: from amphora-aged, copper-coloured Watchtower (a blend of organic Pinot Noir and Pinot Meunier from Hampshire and Devon) to fun and fizzy pét-nats. The wines may be a little offbeat – but all the better for it.

VISIT
Offbeat Wines
Botley's Farm
Downton
Wiltshire
SP5 3NW

SOCIAL
@offbeatwine

WEBSITE
offbeatwines.co.uk

BOTTLE OF NOTE:

WILD JUICE CHASE (TRIOMPHE)
An old vine Triomphe pét-nat. Three weeks of semi-carbonic maceration, fermented in neutral Burgundy barrels, gives this mineral light fizz notes of sappy red fruit, cherry and bramble.

ABOVE AND TOP:
Removing grape skins
after pressing in the
Coquard press.

RIGHT:
Hugo Stewart (left)
and Dan Ham sample
a young wine. They
work collaboratively
on Domaine Hugo, a
traditional-method
sparkling.

The Englishman rolling up his shirtsleeves and hand-picking the finest grapes

The English Winemaker

Clad in tartan with a tweed waistcoat and round glasses, winemaker Matt Gregory looks every bit the geography teacher – his signature moustache adding the final flourish. This is not entirely a coincidence. It was while studying for his geography degree that he discovered a passion for climate science and ecology and first knew that, one day, he wanted to make something from the land himself. So, in 2020, after more than 20 years working as a wine merchant and then a winemaker in New Zealand, Matt took over his first vineyard.

RIGHT:
Winemaker Matt
Gregory next to a
pneumatic grape press
in his winery in the
Leicestershire Wolds.

The vineyard, Walton Brook, lies on the Leicestershire Wolds deep in the farming heartlands, far from traditional winemaking territory. 'It's more of an elaborate ditch than a brook,' Matt says wryly. But he saw potential in the five acre vineyard, and embraced the challenge of converting it to organic farming. Originally planted in 2009, the vineyard had been farmed with conventional, industrial methods for over a decade before Matt came along. To restore the health of the soil, he changed all the processes of the vineyard from the ground up, immediately banning all chemicals. 'Where they hacked and chopped and mowed and sprayed, we now use gentler methods,' Matt says. 'In the spring the whole place is yellow with dandelions, and then goes white with flowering seed heads, and then the daisies come.'

'We've got 200-million-year-old Jurassic limestone, made up from coral and shell, and glacial deposits, as well as really fine minerals like limestone, flint, quartz... It's all there, all the good stuff.'

MATT GREGORY

'I had to farm it with my heart,' he says, 'But we'll never get organic certification here.' Neighbouring industrial farms mean that they'll never be completely free from traces of pesticides and fertilisers, even if Matt would never use them himself, but some things are more important than paperwork, like the wildflowers growing between the vines – a clear sign of life revitalised.

Matt grows a range of grapes from modern hybrids, on this south-facing plot, painting a picture of their myriad 'personalities' as we pace the different blocks: 'Madeline Angevine is quite fun, makes quite zappy, fruity, zippy wine. The Solaris is mental – insanely vigorous and aromatic. It is softer in acidity, really aromatic. Whereas Seyval is a bit grapefruity.'

Until 2021, some of these modern, hybrid varieties were not permitted for use in the production of high-quality, protected designation wines in France and other traditional winemaking regions who regulate which grapes can and cannot be used in order to maintain their reputation. It is,

in many ways, the eagerness of British winemakers like Matt to embrace and experiment with these modern vines that makes their wine so compelling. But he also grows some beloved classics, like the grape he plucks next, pinky-grey in colour, 'Pinot Gris is beautiful, pretty, bright, it's pure.' There are red grapes too. 'Pinot Noir,' he says, 'just seems to love the dirt here. All those things that are supposed to be true about this grape variety, like, it's really hard to grow in the UK and it doesn't want to ripen and it just wants to die all the time... We don't seem to have that.'

The Pinot Noir isn't the only thing that loves the dirt. Matt grabs handfuls of soil and, rubbing it between his fingers, reveals its different textures. 'We've got 200-million-year-old Jurassic limestone, made up from coral and shell, and glacial deposits, as well as really fine minerals like limestone, flint, quartz... It's all there, all the good stuff, all the lovely dirt.'

The farmland that Matt is so passionate about is captured on the labels of his wines. The Ancestral Red, a lightly fizzy blend of Pinot Noir and Pinot Gris, full of freshly crushed cherry and pressed raspberry and sloes, is delicious with charcuterie, and spectacular with the famed pork pies from Melton Mowbray, a fellow Leicestershire neighbour.

LEFT:
Whole bunches of Bacchus ferment during carbonic maceration in their own pressed juice.

205

'Where they hacked and chopped and mowed and sprayed, we now use gentler methods. In the spring the whole place is yellow with dandelions, and then goes white with flowering seed heads, and then the daisies come.'

MATT GREGORY

Then there is the sought-after Field Blend, a blend of both white and red grapes: Seyval, Solaris, Bacchus, Regent, Pinot Noir and Pinot Gris that glows a deep rhubarb pink. Exact varieties and blends vary from year to year, depending on what the vines have to offer, but each promises to be a unique expression of the land and its bounty. While most blended wines today combine grapes harvested from different sites (and sometimes even fermented in different wineries), field blends follow a much older, pre-industrial model in which different varieties are grown together in the same vineyard, or even the same field. Now less common, it is increasingly popular with ecologically minded farmers as diverse planting is always better for local wildlife. Breaking the mould of conventional style, Matt Gregory's wines are low-intervention and at the lively, even funky, end of the spectrum – but to many sommeliers, this is exactly where the future lies.

VISIT
The English Winemaker
Burton-on-the-Wolds
Loughborough
Leicestershire
LE12 5TQ

SOCIAL
@mattgregorywines

WEBSITE
theenglishwinemaker.co.uk

BOTTLES OF NOTE:

THE ANCESTRAL PINK (PINOT NOIR, PINOT GRIS AND BACCHUS), 2021
Notes of strawberry shoelaces, cherryade and spring hedgerow flowers. The grapes were carbonically macerated separately for ten days before being pressed.

THE ANCESTRAL RED (PINOT NOIR AND PINOT GRIS), 2021
The grapes were de-stemmed, crushed and fermented together. It is red and it is fizzy. Flavour-wise, it is an English autumnal country walk (hips, haws, sloes) in a glass.

TOP:
Matt tends to one of the vines on his five acre vineyard, Walton Brook.

MIDDLE:
Atop Matt's Land Rover sits a bottle of his Field Blend, an unfiltered and unfined single vineyard wine made from hand-picked grapes at Walton Brook.

BOTTOM:
Matt with his daughter, Holly, an instrumental member of the team during harvest and in the winery.

Celebrated restaurant with a wine list as locally sourced as the tasting menu

The Ethicurean

Only half an hour's drive outside Bristol, The Ethicurean is a Michelin Green Star restaurant (the highest accolade for sustainable gastronomy) nestled in an 18th-century kitchen garden and old potting shed, overlooking the wooded valleys of the Mendip Hills. Once crumbling and abandoned, the Barley Wood Walled Garden was restored in the early 1990s and is now the setting for a unique culinary experience that celebrates local produce and, crucially, local wines. Sourcing exclusively from the kitchen garden and surrounding hills,

RIGHT:
A bottle of Artefact from Castlewood Vineyard in Devon, made from Bacchus, is served with sourdough and cultured butter.

The Ethicurean is truly the dream for anyone who loves to eat local.

'We work with whatever's growing right now,' head chef and co-owner Mark McCabe explains. 'When things are not just seasonal, but hyper-seasonal, it means that ingredients and produce are sometimes only available for a day or two. The gardener might arrive with a crate of fresh broccoli that's just been picked, and it has to go on the menu today.'

The restaurant's ethos is guided by what Mark and the team describe as a 'sense of place' – the idea that everything is connected with the local area, its history and community. 'It's a distillation of the land,' Mark says, 'and it's about following that flow of flavours across the year.'

'It's very much a philosophy of looking out the window and seeing what's there,' Emily Shephard,

210

ABOVE:
Emily Shephard,
restaurant manager
and wine buyer, with
head chef and co-owner
Mark McCabe.

RIGHT:
The British wines
on their list include
Somerset-based
Dunleavy's (p.172) Bottom
and Sparkling Red.

the restaurant's manager and wine buyer, agrees. It's an attitude that extends to the wine list: 'Over there, by the folly on the hill,' she points, 'is Aldwick Estate.'

Aldwick Estate vineyard and winery produces one of a number of British wines on the list that the team sources from nearby. Emily pours a glass of Bacchus – it has a bright, mouth-filling acidity with exuberant green apple and wild herbs. I find myself thinking that it tastes, somehow, just like the view.

All around the word, wine can be embedded in its region not just in terms of its geography and terroir, but also where it can be best enjoyed – a glass of ballet-slipper pink rosé in the south of France, or a sprightly Vinho Verde on the coast of northern Portugal. Drinking a glass of the local Aldwick Bacchus here, looking out on a wide swathe of English countryside, creates a kind of alchemy, an experience that feels both new in England, and yet like it should have been there all along.

'Funny, isn't it? We're so far removed from where our produce comes from, that people have to be reminded.' Emily adds. The Ethicurean is, in that sense, a blast of fresh air, advocating for ethically sourced wines that are generally organic-leaning and low intervention. 'We don't get too hung up on certification – the good thing about being so local is that you can just pop down the road and see what they're doing.'

Emily and her team are happy to support growers they know are working kindly. Across farming and grape growing, some producers act organically but don't get certified – it's a highly bureaucratic process and not all ethical winemakers are bureaucratic people. Others might be mostly organic, but want to reserve the right to make a few choices – in England it's a hard decision to make, if it's the difference between losing an entire crop or losing organic certification.

When exploring the English wines on their menu, the concept of the 'distillation of the land' returns. For pairings, 'It's that classic thing of "what grows together, goes together,"' explains Emily. There's a reason why high acid, low tannin reds from northern Italy go so well with the tomato passata of their regional pasta dishes, or how delicious a searing, crisp Loire Valley white wine can be when paired with the local Valençay goats cheese. English whites might perhaps be characterised by elderflower, apple and herbaceous notes, and so work outrageously well with produce from The Ethicurean's garden, particularly with late spring crops like broad beans and radishes.

'For earthier dishes later in the year, I'll look to something like Castlewood's Artefact, a skin-contact Bacchus, which has been aged in amphora pots on the grape skins so the wine has soaked up some of the skins' texture and colour.' As hyper-seasonality is the hallmark of The Ethicurean, the menu changes frequently and this means Emily has the chance to get creative with pairings. 'Some seasons are more bountiful than others, so there can be trials and tribulations. Wines will need to be swapped and changed, it's not just going to be a static list. You need to be adaptable to what the grapes are doing and how that works with the food.'

Winemakers often talk about how each bottle represents a stamp in time – how every spring frost or drop of summer rain of the vintage will have shaped the taste of the liquid of that vintage, and no two years will ever be the same. Looking out over the Ethicurean garden, knowing that what's visible today might have gone for the season by tomorrow, gives an appreciation for these flashes of brilliance, whether in the glass or on the table.

Glossary

Winemaking is an art and a science that draws on techniques from
all over the world, but once you know a few key words, it's easy drinking.

AERATION

Most red wines will benefit from a little contact with air to open up the aromas. This can be done by decanting a wine, or simply swilling it around in the glass a little.

AMPHORA

Ceramic vessels used to age and store wine. This method has been around for millennia, but it is increasingly popular with winemakers today.

APPELLATION

A legally defined and protected area, like Champagne. To earn an appellation on their labels, winemakers must obey the strict rules of that specific area (which often concern what varieties can be planted and the minimum alcohol content).

AUTOLYSIS

When the yeast cells break down into lees (dead yeast cells) they produce amino acids and release proteins and carbohydrates into the wine that produce a rich, creamy flavour as well as a distinctive toastiness.

BARRIQUE

Large oak barrels used to store and age wines. Depending on the size and age of the barrel, they can impart distinctly spicy, rich or vanilla flavours.

BIODYNAMIC FARMING

An agricultural method that involves following a holistic view where the vineyard, land and planet are considered as one, and practices are carried out in accordance with the lunar calendar.

BLEND

A wine made from one or more grape varieties (or even batches of wine). Châteauneuf-du-Pape and, quite often, Champagne, for instance, are made from blends.

BRUT

In French the term 'Brut' on wine labels is an indicator of low sugar levels, or 'dry' wine, alternative to the slightly sweeter 'Sec' and 'Demi-sec' which is commonly used to describe Champagne.

CARBONIC MACERATION

A technique used to produce fruity, light red wines. Grapes are fermented whole and uncrushed so that the fermentation begins inside the unbroken grapes and fewer tannins are extracted.

CHAPTALISATION

The process of adding sugar to increase the alcohol content prior to fermentation. It allows winemakers to use less ripened grapes, although it is not legal in every region.

COL FONDO

An Italian sparkling wine whose name translates to 'with the bottom'. It is a cloudy variant of Prosecco, bottled with lees and left undisgorged.

CUVÉE

In sparkling wine, cuvée refers to the best, purest juice pressed from the grapes. So, a cuvée champagne (or even Grand Cuvée) is the best of the vintage. In general winemaking terms, though, it just signals a particular blend, whether of vintages or varieties.

ENOLOGY

The science of wine and winemaking, as opposed to viticulture which is the study of grape cultivation.

FERMENTATION

This process refers to the conversion of grape sugars to alcohol by yeast.

FIELD BLEND

A vineyard planted with different varieties of grape, which are then harvested together to produce a single wine.

FILTRATION

Wine is passed through a filter to remove residual sugars, yeasts and other particles that form a fine sediment. This prevents cloudiness and helps to stabilise the wine. Unfiltered wine can be rested so that sediment settles to the bottom and can be siphoned off if desired.

FINING

A method of clarifying the wine to remove the smallest of particles, preventing hazy wine to produce a bright clear liquid. Often carried out using egg albumen, fish isinglass or gelatin, although vegan alternatives are being developed. Many winemakers choose not to filter or fine their wines.

FINISH

The flavours that linger in the mouth after the wine is tasted. The best wines have long and complex finishes.

FLOR

A film of yeast that forms on the surface of a wine exposed to the air, typically in the production of sherry or Vin Jaune from Jura. To encourage this yeast, barrels are only partly filled.

HYBRID (OR MODERN) VARIETIES

A grape variety made by crossing two different species, typically the European grapevine and the North American grapevine. They are hardier and better suited to cooler climates, but have suffered from an image problem with purists preferring to work with so-called 'noble' varieties. The rise of low-intervention winemaking has helped to boost their reputation, as they require less in terms of sprays, management and labour.

INTERNATIONAL (OR NOBLE) VARIETIES

Vines with a well-known, long-established reputation for producing excellent wines and have consequently been planted far and wide, like Pinot Noir or Chardonnay. These classic varieties often originate from France, although Italian, Spanish and German varieties are also included in their ranks.

LEES

Residual dead yeast particles left over from fermentation, which can if desired be left in contact with the wine during ageing in barrel or in the bottle to add a fuller texture and toasty flavour.

LOW-INTERVENTION WINE

Wine produced with minimal additives or industrial processes (usually commercial yeasts, oak chips, sulphites or fining agents). These 'extras' help to prevent wine from spoiling, so low-intervention winemaking is much riskier, but is preferred for ecological benefits and purity of expression of the fruit. Also known as natural wine.

MALOLACTIC FERMENTATION

The process by which sharp malic acid is converted to creamier, softer lactic acid. It reduces the acidity in wine.

NATURAL WINE

Also known as low-intervention wine, natural wine is made with little-to-no chemical intervention from grapes grown with little-to-no chemical intervention.

NÉGOCIANT

A wine merchant or wholesaler who purchases grapes or wine in bulk from vineyards and bottles the wine to sell on. Négociant winemakers will buy in grapes from vineyards to make wine.

OLD VINE

A term used to describe wines produced from vines typically older than 20 years. Vines can reach 40, 60, or even 100 years. As they age, they produce fewer grapes, but those grapes tend to be more concentrated in flavour.

ORANGE WINE

Also known as skin-contact, orange wines are essentially white wines that are treated like red wines. That is, fermented with the grape skins and seeds intact, so that colour, body and tannins are extracted. The wines will take on a deeper hue, from pale gold through to deep amber, hence the name.

OXIDATION

Oxidation refers to the interaction between oxygen and the liquid, and occurs when wine is stored in a porous vessel like an oak barrel or clay qvevri, A minimal touch of oxidation can contribute richer, fruitier flavours, but too much can lead to undesirable qualities and faults.

PÉT-NATS

Short for *pétillant naturel*, which translates to 'naturally sparkling'. Pét-nat wines are more gentle in their fizz, which occurs due to the wines being bottled part-way through fermentation, trapping the resulting energy from the process, which is absorbed as bubbles. The process also means they are often cloudy. Although a newish trend, it is the original (or 'ancestral') method of creating sparkling wine.

PRESS

Grapes are pressed to release the juice, which can then be taken straight for fermentation, as with most white wines; or the juice can be left to macerate on the skins to absorb extra colour, flavour and tannins, before fermentation, as with red wines and orange wines.

QVEVRI

Large, oval clay pots used by Georgian winemakers for centuries to ferment and age wine, also known as amphora. They are buried in the ground up to the neck to keep them at a constant temperature.

RACKING

The transfer of wine from one vessel to another, either for ageing of the liquid if racked into oak barriques, or to remove sediment (for instance, after fermentation is complete), or separate the wine from the lees or oxidise the wine.

REGENERATIVE FARMING

A general term for an agricultural method that focuses on conservation and rehabilitation, particularly topsoil, water cycle and biodiversity.

ROSÉ

Red grapes are crushed with their skins for just a short time before the skins are discarded (whereas, to make red wine the skins are left in throughout fermentation). The longer the skins remain, the deeper the pink.

SKIN-CONTACT WINE

Also known as orange wine, skin-contact wines are white wines fermented with grape skins and seed left in to add flavour, body and tannin. The method is ancient and originates in Georgia.

SOMMELIER

A highly-trained and knowledgeable wine professional responsible for aspects of wine service, list curation and pairings. Once found only in fine dining, the new wave of wine culture has given rise to a new breed of sommelier (or 'somm') working from more casual wine bars.

SULPHITES (SO2)

Typically used to prevent oxidation and keep bacteria at bay, use of sulphur is rejected by natural winemakers as it can limit a wine's complexity and range of flavours. Sulphites have been used for centuries and can also occur naturally in wine.

TANNINS

Derived from grape skins, seed and stems, tannins make your mouth pucker when you drink a glass of red wine. They also act as a natural preservative to help the wine age and develop.

TERROIR

The interaction of soil, climate, topography and grape variety which makes wine from a specific site distinct.

TRADITIONAL-METHOD SPARKLING

Time and labour-intensive method used to proceed Champagne, Cava and other high-quality sparkling wines. Involves a sugar and yeast-induced second fermentation to a 'complete' wine inside the bottle, which in turn requires a tricky rotation, removal and refill process afterwards.

VIGNERON

A farmer who grows grapes for winemaking.

VINTAGE

A vintage refers to the year in which the grapes were grown and harvested. Vintage variation refers to the differing properties that grapes will have in light of different weather conditions. For instance, hot years may produce more sugar, while cool years might mean more fresh flavours.

VITICULTURE

The cultivation, science and study of grapes, as opposed to enology which is the study of winemaking.

WINERY

A place where wine is made, often attached to a vineyard but not always.

WILD FERMENTATION

Yeast is responsible for converting the sugars in grapes into alcohol (and carbon dioxide), turning otherwise sweet and simple grape juice into wine. Winemakers can use cultured yeast parcels developed specifically for wine fermentation, or they can allow the native yeasts in the environment to do this. Following this approach gives the winemaker less control over the final outcome of the wine, and may result in surprising or unexpected flavours and aromas.

YEAST

Added during winemaking to kickstart fermentation and convert sugar to alcohol. Low-intervention winemakers use native (or wild) yeasts, which occur naturally on the grapes but are much less reliable than commercially cultured yeasts.

Key Stockists

Some of the best places to get your hands on a bottle (or three) of British wine.

ANOTHER HEART TO FEED,
MANCHESTER
anotherhearttofeed.co.uk
In-person.

BERRY BROS & RUDD,
PALL MALL & BASINGSTOKE
bbr.com
In-person and online.

BOTTLE CHOP, LEEDS
bottlechop.co.uk
In-person and online.

CAMBRIDGE WINE MERCHANTS,
CAMBRIDGE
cambridgewine.com
In-person and online.

EMERGING VINES
emergingvines.co.uk
Online.

FOREST WINES, WALTHAMSTOW
forestwines.com
In-person and online.

FRANKLIN'S WINE, NOTTING HILL
Franklinswine.com
In-person.

FUTTLE, FIFE
futtle.com
In-person and online.

GRACE + JAMES, BIRMINGHAM
graceandjames.xyz
In-person.

GRAPE BRITANNIA, CAMBRIDGE
grapebritannia.co.uk
In-person and online.

IDLE MOMENTS, HACKNEY
idle-moments.com
In-person and online.

JUICED WINES
juicedwines.co.uk
Online.

KERB, MANCHESTER
kerb.wine
In-person and online.

KORK WINE AND DELI,
NEWCASTLE UPON TYNE
korkwineanddeli.com
In-person and online.

LES CAVES DE PYRENE
shop.lescaves.co.uk
Online.

LITTLE RASCAL, EDINBURGH
littlerascalwine.co.uk
In-person and online.

LOKI WINE, BIRMINGHAM
lokiwine.co.uk
In-person and online.

LOW INTERVENTION
lowintervention.com
Online.

MADE FROM GRAPES, GLASGOW
madefromgrapes.shop
In-person and online.

MONTY WINES, BRISTOL
montywines.co.uk
Online.

MOTHER SUPERIOR, NUNHEAD
mothersuperior.co.uk
In-person and online.

NATTY BOY WINES, BATTERSEA
nattyboywines.co.uk
In-person at sister bar
Dan's and online.

NEW BREED, ESSEX
newbreedbottleshop.com
In-person and online.

NOBLE FINE LIQUOR, HACKNEY
noblefineliquor.co.uk
In-person and online.

ORANJ
oranj.co.uk
Online.

PECKHAM CELLARS, PECKHAM
peckhamcellars.co.uk
In-person and online.

QUALITY WINES, FARRINGDON
qualitywinesfarringdon.com
In-person.

SHRINE TO THE VINE, HOLBORN
shrinetothevine.co.uk
In-person and online.

SIP WINES
sipwines.shop
Online.

THE ENGLISH VINE
theenglishvine.co.uk
Online.

THE WINE SOCIETY
thewinesociety.com
Online.

UNCHARTED WINES
unchartedwines.com
Online.

UNDER THE BONNET WINES
www.winesutb.com
Online.

VAGABOND,
MULTIPLE ACROSS LONDON
vagabondwines.co.uk
In-person and online.

VINO VERO, LEIGH-ON-SEA
vinovero.co.uk
In-person and online.

WAYWARD WINES, LEEDS
waywardwines.co.uk
In-person and online.

WEINO BIB, HACKNEY
weinobib.co.uk
In-person and online.

WINE & GREENE, TOTNES
wineandgreene.com
In-person and online.

WOLF WINE, BATH
wolfwine.co.uk
In-person and online.

WRIGHTS, CARMARTHENSHIRE
shop.wrightsfood.co.uk
In-person and online.

Acknowledgements

A huge thank you to everyone for letting us come scrabble around in various vineyards, wineries, bars and restaurants – for the delicious and very generous tastings of so many wonderful wines, and for the uplifting, inspiring, thought-provoking chats among the vines, in woodland meadows, around campfires and kitchen tables and tucked away in corners of dining rooms. Thanks for sharing a piece of your journey – I have loved writing everything up and being able to relive our conversations all over again. I feel very honoured to be bringing some of these stories out into the world.

There's so much more to the wine industry than what we see on the surface; there's a lot that goes on behind the scenes. To everyone picking grapes, packing boxes, delivering bottles, pouring glasses and everything in between – a great big cheers from all of us.

With thanks to Emma, Steph, Rhea, Hugo, Steve and the Fisheries family. Thank you to Rosie, Laura, Clara, Sophie, Holly, Sarah, Teila; to Ariana; and to Maria, for beautiful photos and an excellent selection of car snacks.

A massive thanks to the small but incredibly mighty Hoxton Mini Press team for everything: Octavia, Rich, Florence, Martin and Ann, and Beca, whose brilliant idea inspired this book.

ABOVE:
A team of grape pickers at Botley Farm in Wiltshire, where Offbeat (p.196) has its winery. One of the most important, yet often unseen, jobs in the wine industry.